Frances Tenenbaum, Series Editor

HOUGHTON MIFFLIN COMPANY
Boston • New York   1998

Garden Paths

A new way to solve practical problems in the garden

GORDON HAYWARD

Taylor's Guide is a registered trademark of Houghton Mifflin Company.

Library of Congress Cataloging-in-Publication Data

Hayward, Gordon.
    Garden paths : a new way to solve practical problems in the garden / Gordon Hayward.
        p. cm. — (Taylor's weekend gardening guides)
    ISBN 0-395-82493-7
    1. Garden walks — Design and construction — Amateurs' manuals. 2. Landscape
gardening — Amateurs' manuals.   I. Title. II. Series.
    TH4970.H38 1998
    712 — dc21   98-11765

Printed in the United States of America.

WCT 10 9 8 7 6 5 4 3 2 1

Book design by Deborah Fillion
Drawings by Elayne Sears
Cover photograph © by Jerry Pavia

CONTENTS

I.

Paths: Where to Put Them,
How to Make Them

Paths are practical. They take you and your guests from one point to another in your garden on a solid footing. They provide access for you and your tools. They reduce maintenance by helping to control surface drainage, weeds, mud, heat, and dust. But they also do a lot more. They draw people into your garden and, in a very real way, lead them through it.

Well-designed paths are irresistible. They invite people to explore. Put a curve in a path that disappears around a corner and visitors will yearn to know what is around that corner. If that path leads to other thoughtfully designed paths, your garden, no matter how big or small, will become a coherent whole while offering intrigue, surprise, movement, variety, and ever-changing perspectives.

Paths can also be the way to solve many design problems you might confront:

- You want to create a really wonderful garden around the front door. Where do you begin?
- You've just built a house and moved in. Where do you begin your garden design, and once started, how do you develop it?
- You have a garden with a bit of this and a bit of that. How can you pull all these unrelated parts together into a whole?
- You are bored with the foundation planting along the front of your home. Is there an alternative?
- You have a tiny garden. How can you make it feel bigger?
- You love perennial beds, but you don't know where to put them.

The path, then, is certainly a way to get from point A to point B on solid ground, but it is also a way to answer any number of practical gardening concerns.

CHAPTER 1

WELCOME TO OUR HOME

I t is helpful to think about paths in order of their importance to your garden. For example, the path that people follow from the driveway or the street to the front door is the most important or primary path. It sets the tone for your garden and your home by welcoming visitors, directing them to the appropriate door, and helping them feel that they have arrived at a private space separate from the world. Another primary path might lead from your back door into your back-yard. This path is the beginning of your itinerary through your garden, and it serves as a kind of hub from which secondary and tertiary paths lead.

Secondary paths are narrower and direct people from broad primary paths to less important paths — for example, down the side of the house. Secondary paths might also lead from the back primary path to a little pool, an herb garden, or the vegetable garden. Tertiary paths, the narrowest of all, might go through the vegetable garden to the compost pile, or from the little pool into a bit of wood-land or a nearby grape arbor.

Cut stone is most appropriate for a broad path to the front door of a formal or modern home. Secondary paths can lead off to the right or left of the entrance garden to form the spine of side and back gardens.

Once you determine where your paths will go and whether they are primary, secondary, or tertiary, you have a basis on which to decide how wide they should be and whether they should be straight or curving. This pares down the list of materials appropriate for each one. In the very broadest sense, the most formal materials belong near the house, less formal ones are best in the middle ground of your garden, and the least formal ones work at the edges or in practical areas such as the vegetable garden.

The term "visual weight" is useful in understanding why this is so. The primary paths should have the most visual weight — that is, they must catch the eye most readily — and the tertiary paths the least. The front primary path is the widest, most welcoming path in your design. If two paths are in view as guests arrive and they sometimes take the wrong one, you need to add visual weight to the primary path with lighting, planted pots, plantings, garden sculpture, fences and gates, or an arbor through which to walk. The secondary path — say the one from the garage door to the kitchen door — needs to be reduced in visual weight, by making it narrower, using a less formal material, or removing details that attract visitors' eyes. The visual weight of tertiary paths is even less; for instance, these might be barely visible trodden earth paths to direct your guests through the woods in your backyard.

THE PRIMARY PATH

The most important path in your garden is the one that directs people to the front door. This is the path where the design for a garden should begin.

The primary path has to be the widest path on your property, and certainly the most welcoming one your guests see when they arrive. Its width should be determined by the width of some architectural element near the front door, so the house and the path relate to each other. Take a tape measure and see what width seems most appropriate: the front door and its trim, the front porch, or perhaps wooden or stone steps. These elements usually call for a path that is three and a half to six feet wide. Use garden hoses or strings tied to bamboo stakes to try out a variety of widths to get it right.

Besides width, you need to decide whether the path should be straight or curving. Straight paths are typically more formal, and their direction is easier to deter-

Fieldstones work well in a primary path to the front door, especially if they are laid tightly against one another to provide predictable footing. The color of these sandstones is nicely offset by the variegated plants in the entrance garden.

mine. It's trickier to make a curving path, because the curve has to go around something to look right. To establish visual logic, don't make a curving path just for the sake of the curve; instead, run it around the trunk of an existing tree or plant a tree or a flower bed to provide a reason for the curve.

Keep in mind that the primary path must be practical as well as inviting. People don't want to carry luggage on a path that meanders, and they don't want to feel that they have to look down to see where to put their feet next. Be straight and to the point. Get people where they want to go with a path that is three to six feet wide and that has a uniform and predictable surface.

The main path should provide a feeling of entrance, too. A lamppost, potted plants, beds, a fence with a gate through it — any of these elements will help establish that this is the primary path. Once people arrive at your front door, the path might widen into a generous landing, where you can set planted pots by way of a greeting.

Because you want this path to be safe, predictable, and welcoming, it must be made from a material that can be set firmly in place. Cut stone, brick, or very large stepping stones set close together are your best options. All of these can also be used for steps. (If you choose to construct brick steps, make the tread — what you put your foot on — of cut stone or fieldstone and the risers — what the treads sit on — of brick. Only bricks set in mortar will stay in place in a set of steps.) When deciding on the material for your primary path, don't consider gravel or crushed stone, since people will track these materials into your house and onto carpets and floors.

Another primary path might be a broad swath of lawn that runs from the back door between rows of trees or perennial borders out into the garden. A primary path might also lead directly from a main door of the house to an outbuilding, a guesthouse, or an arbor set among trees at the back of your property.

SECONDARY PATHS

It is often a good idea to have subordinate paths leading off a primary path. For example, let's say you have decided to make a five-foot-wide brick path to the front door. About six feet before you get to the step into the house, you might add a secondary brick path, only about two feet wide, that leads along the front

This wide brick path narrows just past the entrance to form a secondary path that leads along the front and around to gardens at the side. It doubles as an edging for the beds next to the house.

Broad stepping stones running through the low plantings of the surrounding garden contribute to the informal mood of this rustic home. Narrower stepping-stone paths can lead to other parts of the garden or other outbuildings.

and then down the side of your house. If you live in a rural area, you might make an informal two-foot-wide stepping-stone path that goes along the front and out to a vegetable or cutting garden. Such secondary paths invite visitors to walk along the front of the house and then explore the gardens at the sides.

A secondary path is invariably narrower than the primary path, and it is often made with a less formal material, or with the same material laid in a visually lighter way. For instance, if the primary path is five feet wide and made of tightly laid cut stones, then you can lay the same cut stone in two-foot widths to make a secondary path. If the primary path is straight and formal, the secondary path might curve. Secondary paths can also be used as edging, leading people along the side of a garden or into a garden which they can appreciate from either side.

Small fieldstones laid tightly together make this narrow secondary path fit with the proportions of this long, narrow space. Plants in profusion then predominate to create a welcoming side garden.

TERTIARY PATHS

Once you go around the front corner and down the side of the house on a secondary path, you might see possibilities for tertiary paths. These can lead into a vegetable garden or a compost area behind the garage, or into the woodland between your house and your neighbor's. As we have noted, tertiary paths are the narrowest ones and call for the least formal materials. Stepping stones, gravel, pine needles, or bark mulch may be just right. If you have a two-foot-wide step-

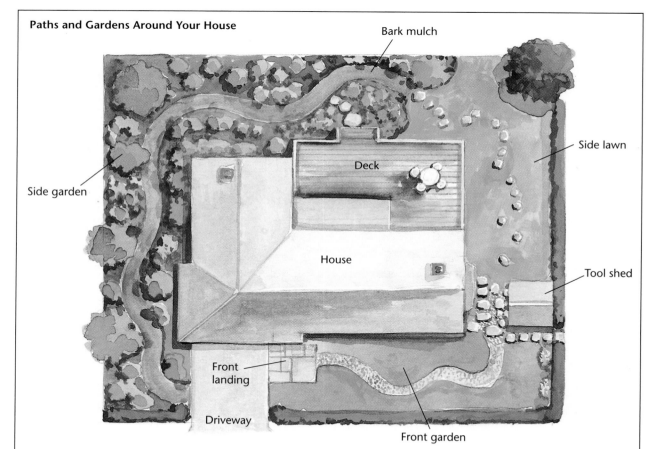

Paths and Gardens Around Your House

Bark mulch

Side lawn

Side garden

Deck

House

Tool shed

Front landing

Driveway

Front garden

Paths, and thus gardens, can surround your house. Change the paving materials to change the mood by using cut stone formally for the front steps and landing and informally as a useful landing by the tool shed. Use stepping stones through the side lawn and out from the deck and a crushed gravel path meandering through the informal front garden. Bark mulch is appropriate through the rustic wooded side garden.

Gardening Between the House and an Outbuilding

The space between the garage and the side door of the house is a perfect place for a formal enclosed garden. The side doors of the two buildings are good starting places for the secondary path. The main path can run from the sidewalk and through the formal garden to the back gardens.

ping-stone path running along the side of your house, for example, you might use bark mulch to create a twelve- to sixteen-inch-wide path that goes behind the garage and into the vegetable garden.

TRANSITIONS BETWEEN PATHS

If you are using two different materials for your paths, it is sometimes helpful to introduce a third to make the transition more visually pleasing. Say you have a secondary lawn path that leads to a tertiary bark-mulch path into the woods. If you place a stepping stone across both paths where they join, it will act as a kind of link between the two materials. The result is a more graceful transition.

A path can serve as the basis for designing an exciting garden between the driveway and the front door. Here stepping stones have been used to make a curving path up to the porch. The boulder at the beginning of the curve makes the shape seem logical.

Steps are also a good way to make a transition from one material to another. You might have a secondary path of brick that leads up fieldstone steps with brick risers to a stepping-stone path into a cutting garden. Another possibility is to run a tightly laid cut-stone path between two perennial beds and then, when you come to the end of the beds and you want to lead people toward the woods, gradually set the stones further and further apart, until they become individual stepping stones that lead onto the bark-mulch path. Good transitions between paths and paving materials ensure that your garden is presented as a gentle experience.

MAKING THE FIRST DECISIONS

There are several things to keep in mind when deciding what materials to use for your paths. First, consider what the architecture of your house calls for. If you have an old clapboard farmhouse, you will choose less formal materials than someone who lives in a fine suburban home or a formal brick colonial. You also need to understand how practical the materials will be in terms of maintenance and utility, and whether or not you want to lay the paths yourself or hire a professional. Finally, remember that the materials you choose for your paths should underpin the feeling of the gardens through which they lead. Once the gardens are established and full, the paths and their materials will recede into the background, having provided a design structure and an itinerary.

CHAPTER 2
CHOOSING MATERIALS

A number of materials are appropriate for making paths. Before deciding which ones to use, take time to decide how you want each garden space to feel and how quickly you want people to move through it. Take a close look at your house. Is it formal or informal? Urban, suburban, or rural? What color is it, and how could the color of the paths help link your house to your garden?

Also think about how each path will be used. For example, a wide cut-stone path feels formal and moves people through space quickly. A stepping-stone path has a more informal feel and leads people slowly along, because they have to take time to see where to take their next step. A pine-needle path is ideal for strolling slowly through quiet woodlands.

After you have thought carefully about what kind of paths you need, consider the following materials and the moods they help create in your garden.

CUT STONE

If you have a formal or traditional home made of stone or white clapboard, the best material to use near the house is cut stone. Depending on where you live,

Stepping stones are a good choice of material when you want to create a relaxed feeling. A variety of plants will thrive in the surrounding soil, integrating the garden and the path.

bluestone, granite, marble, sandstone, or whatever other cut stones are indigenous to your area will be most appropriate for the primary path to the front door. (Avoid slate. Though it is widely available, it has a slippery surface.)

Cut stones, which are invariably square or rectangular, range from one foot square up to about four feet square. They fit tightly together to form straight paths or patios that reflect the geometry of the house and provide a predictable, safe surface on which to walk. Cut stone is the best material to use when the path is essential for getting people directly from one place to another safely, including those in high heels and wheelchairs. They also have the advantage of requiring very little maintenance; because the stones can be laid so tightly, there is little room for weeds to get established.

A cut-stone pathway from the sidewalk or garage to the front door can easily broaden to form a generous landing when it arrives at its destination. A secondary path of cut stone that continues across the front of the house and perhaps down one or both sides does well as an edging material for a three- or four-foot-wide garden next to the foundation. By using the same stone to create walkways, landings, and perhaps a terrace or patio in back, you visually link the straight lines of the house, the paths, and the gardens, creating a harmonious whole.

If you use large stones for your paths, you will probably want to hire a professional to install them. A three-by-three-foot stone is heavy to handle and breaks easily if the base on which it is laid is not uniformly flat, so a knowledgeable and experienced professional can probably do the best job.

BRICK

Brick paths look especially good leading up to brick houses, vacation homes, and small buildings. Because its color is warm and inviting, this material works well with informal gardens, too. Bricks can be used effectively to make secondary paths leading through cottage or vegetable gardens, among herb or rose gardens, or underneath a rustic pergola, and they make a good surface for furniture under a grape arbor.

Because bricks can be cut easily with a brick chisel or a rented brick cutter, it is possible to use them to create a variety of shapes and forms that are impossible, or unsuitable, with cut stone. Though each brick is rectangular, you can lay

By leaving gaps between these cut stones and deciding not to align their ends, the person who made this path gave them a more informal look appropriate for a secondary path.

brick paths to form curves and circles, or in a wide variety of patterns that add visual interest to your garden. Use detailed patterns when you want people to slow down to look at the garden — for instance, when the path runs through a carefully planned knot garden. However, if you just want a functional path between the driveway and the front door, a simple pattern that does not call attention to itself is best.

Bricks can be either handmade or machine-made. Handmade bricks have more character, as they are irregular (some are quite misshapen) and may have patches of plaster on them. When laid in a path, they add interest and create an aura of age, so they are particularly appropriate near an old house. Modern machine-made bricks have less character because they are identical to one another, but they can be laid more tightly than old brick, so weeds and grass have a harder time taking hold in the sandy grouting between and beneath them.

If you need to make steps along a brick path, use cement to hold the bricks together, or use cut stone for the treads and bricks for the risers.

STONE CARPET

A stone carpet is made by laying irregularly shaped fieldstones (also known as flagstones) between ten and thirty-six inches across next to one another. Because the individual stones are sometimes rounded and sometimes straight and they are all of different sizes, this method of creating a path gives you a lot of flexibility.

A stone carpet might be anywhere from eighteen inches to seven feet wide, depending on the scale of the gardens through which it passes. It can also go up and down gentle slopes like a ramp, so you don't need steps. You might lay a stone carpet as an informal primary path to the front door, or as a patio that changes into a path at one side, leading off through adjacent beds to widen out again under an arbor. Another possibility is to make a path that wends its way through a woodland garden, sometimes reaching out to surround the trunk of a tree or leading up to the edge of a boulder. If your lawn includes two island beds that are only a few feet apart, you can replace the sod between the beds with a stone carpet, creating one garden with a stone path through it.

It is easy to manipulate the degree of formality in these paths. If you lay the stones very tightly and create straight edges with a uniform width, the stone carpet will have a formal look. But if you lay the stones so the edges of the path (or

To soften the look of these broad fieldstone steps, the designer backfilled the gaps with sandy loam and set in alpines and other creeping plants.

the gaps between the stones) are irregular, the look will be more casual. You might want to use stepping-stone paths as a transition from the stone carpet to even less formal areas of your garden; for instance, a stone carpet could lead from your patio to a grape arbor thirty feet away on the lawn, with secondary paths of stepping stones leading from the carpet to an herb garden on one side and to a bench set in a perennial border on the other.

To increase the informality of your stone carpet, leave out a stone here and there, backfill the gap with sandy loam rather than the standard base material for the path, and set in small plants that don't mind being walked on, like thyme, ajuga, *Alchemilla pubescens,* or a groundcover.

Because you can choose the size of the stones to use in the path, you might want to lay a stone carpet yourself rather than hire a professional.

GRASS

Lawn grass is the most elegant of all paving materials, but that elegance comes at a price. A grass path requires a lot of maintenance. It has to be mown at least weekly and edged every month or so to keep it from creeping into adjacent beds. If you live in the southern third of the United States, you will also have to install irrigation to keep it looking good, and even then you won't be able to use the fine-bladed grasses found in the beautiful lawns of the Northeast. To flourish, lawn grasses need several hours of direct sunlight a day, so they are not appropriate for paths in shady gardens.

Grass can be useful to make a broad, straight primary path leading from a terrace or patio to an arbor or pergola at the far end of your backyard. A wide, gently curving path of lawn can lead people from one perennial bed to another, or a narrow ribbon of grass can create what feels like a long journey through a small garden.

Because lawn grass is the only living paving material, you should use it only in places where it won't be worn down by the passage of many feet over it. Avoid using it at gateways, or to make paths through small-scale herb or rose gardens, where it would require fussy mowing and edging. And don't rely on grass as the path to the front door or between the frequently used side door and the garage: your shoes will get soaked with dew every morning and evening, and the path will become muddy when it rains.

Given these caveats, lawn grass is a remarkably flexible and handsome paving material. Broad expanses of lawn can narrow down to become four- or five-foot-wide pathways between beds and then broaden out again into lawn, giving the property a coherent look, with the green grass acting as a subtle foil to the colors and forms of nearby perennials and shrubs. Grass can also negotiate gentle slopes, sweeping around corners with ease and rolling up and down existing terrain, or it can broaden and then narrow to add the feeling of movement to your gardens.

If you have a broad expanse of lawn at the back of your house, look at it as a blank slate. Draw curving or repetitive shapes for beds on its surface with hoses, and a garden begins to appear where a visually lifeless rectangle now sits. Or you can sow seed or lay sod to create lawn paths where no lawn now exists. This is work you can easily do yourself.

The stepping stones through this sunny perennial border are surrounded by Hall's woolly thyme. Using a single plant in this way emphasizes the role of the path as the garden's spine.

STEPPING STONES

Stepping-stone paths are made of individual fieldstones laid one after the other through informal areas such as woodland, herb or rock gardens, and wildflower gardens or as maintenance paths through beds. People must walk single file on them, since you move from stone to stone.

Gravel paths can be either free-form, as this one is, or straight. Plants flopping onto the edges of the path pull the garden and the path together visually, and the rose bower creates the feeling of entering a new space.

Stepping stones are the most appropriate material to use if you want to determine the pace at which visitors will enjoy your garden. If you place eighteen-inch-wide fieldstones (a minimum size for a stepping stone) two or three inches apart, people will have to walk slowly, paying attention to what is around them as well as to where they will step next. But if you place those same stones a foot or more apart, you increase the length of the visitors' stride and speed up their pace.

Because stepping stones create relatively narrow paths, it is important that they offer secure footing. Don't set stepping stones on an angle or a slope; set each one level, even when going up a gentle slope. Otherwise you run the risk that visitors' heels will slip on a sloping stone, especially when the stones are wet or covered with frost. And always set the length of the stone, not the width, across the path.

Stepping stones are the perfect material when you want to blur the lines between a path and a garden. Low plants can be set in the gaps between the stones or at their edges, so the garden can wrap right around the stones in the path, creating a visual unity. You can place stepping stones easily on your own.

HARD LOOSE MATERIALS

Gravel, crushed stone, and other crunchy surfaces are an alternative that falls between stone and lawn-grass walkways. Gravel or crushed-stone paths are particularly suitable for herb or vegetable gardens, rock gardens, and informal gardens at the edges of your property, especially in the Southwest, where gravel is prevalent. Gravel paths can also meander through woods or shrubs at the back of your property to increase the feeling of space in a small area. They also offer something no other material can supply: sound. The crunching of small stones against one another tells visitors that they have stepped on a new surface and entered a new space in the garden.

Because they provide plenty of traction, gravel paths can negotiate gentle slopes; if the hill gets too steep for comfortable walking, you can set stepping stones flat into the slope to provide sound footing. But don't use gravel paths near doorways, because the fine particles easily adhere to the soles of your shoes and get tracked into the house.

Crushed-stone paths, especially when laid three to four inches thick, require relatively little maintenance and create an informal feeling in the garden. Floppy

Brick makes a good path through lawn, but when you get to the edge of a woodland, it is best to shift to bark mulch, pine needles, or trodden earth. The meandering curves in this shady garden create a feeling of suspense and draw people on to explore.

perennials like catmint and lady's mantle or sprawling annuals like nasturtiums can fall onto a gravel path and not get clipped by a lawn mower as they would on a grass path. If you want a more formal look, you can edge gravel paths with stone, brick, or wood.

Because gravel or crushed-stone paths are easy to lay, you can make these walkways yourself, following the directions for making a path in chapter 3.

SOFT LOOSE MATERIALS

Bark mulch, pine needles, leaves, and packed earth are the least formal of all the paving materials and are most appropriate at the outer reaches of your garden. Only if you have a rustic log cabin or a weekend house in the mountains should you use any of these materials near the house.

Soft loose materials are perfect to lead people through your vegetable garden or from a shed to the garden and the compost heap. These organic materials are also useful to create informal sitting areas under trees or in the woods. Look at the places at the sides or back of your property where you never go, such as a cluster of trees or shrubs that has always been there but that you've never entered. Cut a path through the brush and lay down a bark-mulch path, or trim the lower branches of the pines and create a pine-needle path under the trees.

Be aware of the fact that these materials are best used to echo the natural surroundings. Don't put a pine-needle path under spruces; it won't look natural. Use bark mulch instead, if spruce needles aren't available. Remember that you are constructing casual, natural-looking paths that are invariably narrow and meandering. Use indigenous material whenever possible, and make the paths yourself.

Chapter 3
Making Paths

Laying paths of stone, lawn grass, or bark mulch is not really a daunting task. With an understanding of how to prepare the base and a willingness to learn how to lay the materials through trial and error, you should be able to make your own paths. The sections that follow explain many of the details you need to know to succeed. If you decide to hire a professional, this information will give you a greater appreciation for his or her work.

The Standard Base

Because good drainage is central to the long-term stability of every path, one of the first things to determine before you begin work on the base is the nature of your soil. If it is sandy or gravelly and water runs through it freely, you won't need to go to great lengths to assure good drainage. However, if it is dense with clay or a heavy topsoil, you will need to construct the base so the path drains well. Similarly, if you live where the soil freezes in the winter or where the soil expands and contracts in wet and dry seasons, you also need to pay careful attention to drainage.

This brick path through a perennial garden passes under a rose-covered arbor to lead people from one garden space to another.

Use the following guidelines for making the ideal base, then alter it based on the nature of the soil and how much work you want to do.

First, define the path by pounding stakes into the ground and tying strings between them to determine the exact width and length of the path. Be sure to measure carefully if you are making a straight, formal path. If you want to create broad curves, use hoses to suggest the outer edges of the walkway and then set stakes every five or six feet to record the edges.

Then, using a shovel or spade, dig along the length of the path to a depth of about a foot, setting aside the soil for later use. If your soil drains particularly poorly, lay down an inch or so of 1½-inch crushed stone. (Be sure to get this size, rather than a finer crushed stone.) Then place a perforated four-inch PVC drainpipe along the center line of the path, laying the perforations down on the crushed stone and being sure that the pipe will drain in the appropriate direction away from the house.

If you don't need to add the drainpipe, backfill the path with four to six inches of 1½-inch crushed stone. To figure out how much stone to order from a sand-and-gravel supplier, first determine how deep the layer will be. Then multiply the

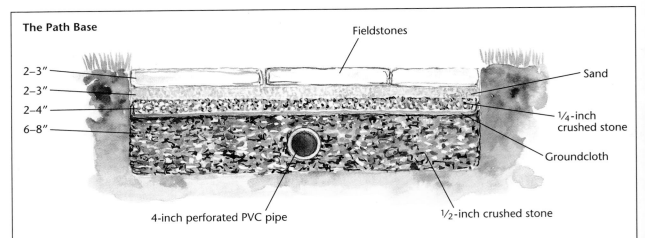

The Path Base

Fieldstones

Sand

2–3″

2–3″

2–4″

6–8″

¼-inch crushed stone

Groundcloth

4-inch perforated PVC pipe

½-inch crushed stone

The base for a path set into poorly drained soil might need all the elements shown here. However, if your soil is sandy or gravelly, you can dispense with the PVC pipe and use considerably less crushed stone under the path.

length of the path (in feet) times the width and multiply the result times the depth of the crushed stone. This will give you the amount in cubic feet. Divide that number by twenty-seven (the number of cubic feet in a cubic yard) to find out how many cubic yards you need to order. For example, if your path is fifteen feet long and four feet wide and you are filling the one-foot-deep trench with six inches of crushed stone, the calculation is $15 \times 4 = 60$, $60 \times .5 = 30$, $30 \div 27 =$ just over one cubic yard.

Once you have backfilled the trench with the crushed stone and raked it to make it level, lay a porous weed barrier or woven black plastic groundcloth on top. This is available in three-, four-, and six-foot widths and can be cut easily with scissors. To finish the base, add two to four inches of finely crushed gravel on top of the cloth and top that with two to four inches of sand, leaving room for the thickness of the paving material you will be using.

Cut-Stone Paths

Of all the paving materials, cut stones require the most expertise to lay; but don't let this fact discourage you. Lay the base, buy stones that are no larger than three feet square, and set to with a will and plenty of patience.

Getting the material. Cut stone is available from masonry suppliers. If you have trouble finding a source, contact a stonemason or building contractor in your area and ask where you can get it. The stones are typically square or rectangular and range in size from one foot square to four feet square, in six-inch increments. They usually cost around three or four dollars a square foot. To determine how much you will need to spend, multiply the length of your path times the width to get the square feet. A fifteen-by-four-foot path would require sixty square feet of stone, at a cost of around $250.

Several types of cut stone are available, depending on where you live. Blue-stone, granite, limestone, and sandstone are the most common choices. Be sure to choose a stone with a texture that shoes will not slide on. For instance, both slate and marble are available, but marble is so smooth it can get slippery when wet, and slate is slick in any weather.

Laying a cut-stone walkway. Once you have built the base for your path as outlined above, you are ready to begin laying the stone itself. If your path leads to or from a building, start next to the building and work toward the other end. If it leads from one building to another, work from both ends toward the middle so you can make adjustments along the way. If the path includes steps, start at the bottom of the slope and work toward the top.

Long slabs of cut stone can be combined with small, tightly set fieldstones to create a traditional Japanese look.

Begin by choosing one of your largest stones to form the threshold stone. This stone should be big enough to draw the eye to the path, and it should promise sound footing. Roughly place the threshold stone and then try out four or five other stones near it to get the feel of how they will look together and how far apart they should be. Don't step on the stones until they are completely supported by the base; many kinds of two-inch-thick stones will readily snap underfoot if they are not properly supported.

If you want the stones to be tightly set, you can butt each one against the next. However, given that the stones are rarely cut perfectly during the manufacturing process, it is usually best to leave one-quarter to one-half inch between them so that they will settle well and so that the path will drain properly. Be sure to place the smaller stones in the interior of the path; if someone steps on a one-foot-square stone at the edge, it may well shift underfoot.

Cut-Stone Patterns

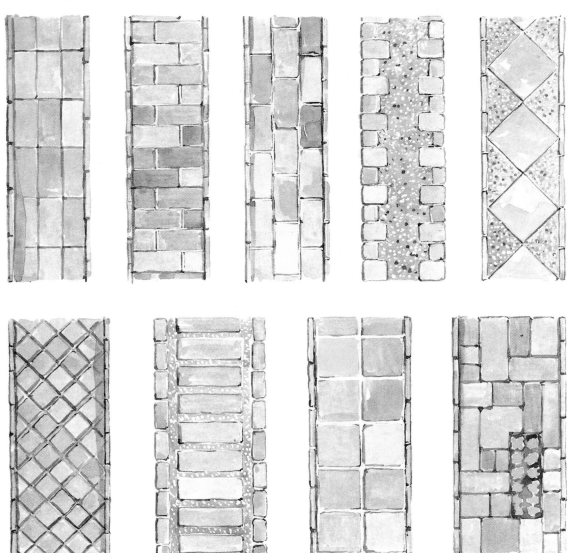

Cut stones can be used in a variety of ways to create interesting patterns on the ground. Use a simple pattern in a complex garden and vice versa for pleasing contrast. Cut stone can also be combined with other materials, such as crushed stone or gravel. Stones laid on the diagonal will require more cutting than those laid parallel to the path.

Base for a Cut-Stone Path on Well-Drained Soil

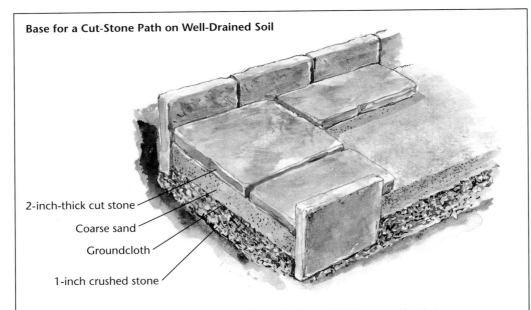

2-inch-thick cut stone

Coarse sand

Groundcloth

1-inch crushed stone

Cut stone can be laid on a few inches of finely crushed gravel. To increase the drainage underneath, you may need to lay two or three inches of 1½-inch crushed stone and then woven black plastic cloth beneath the gravel. The bottom of the edging stones should sit on crushed stone for good drainage.

Once you have laid five or six stones roughly in place, set them by twisting them down into the sand until they are exactly where you want them. Make sure they are level. Then tap each one several times with a rubber mallet to set it firmly and check with a spirit level to be certain it is properly set. Continue laying the stones five or six at a time, setting them and checking the path for bumps or tilts as you go along.

When you have finished laying the walkway, spread sand over its length, sweep the sand into the gaps between the stones, and run a sprinkler over it for ten minutes or so to settle the sand into the joints. You may have to add more sand a few times before it settles to the depth you want: about a quarter of an inch below the tops of the stones. That recess will keep the sand from scattering onto the surface of the path and ending up on people's shoes and thus on your floors and carpets.

Edging the path. If your path runs along the edge of a garden, it is a good idea to use the same stones set on edge to create a low retaining border that separates the garden from the paved surface and prevents the soil from leaching out when it rains. Set one-foot-wide stones on edge, leaving a three- to four-inch relief above the grade of the path; such an edging will not only hold soil in place but also create a neat edge.

Making steps. Starting with the bottom step, build up risers on a crushed-stone base with the paving stones, or use a complementary stone or brick. Lay sections of stone to form the face and sides of the riser, then fill in the resulting space with either crushed stone or stone dust (don't use sand, as rainwater will wash it out between the gaps in the stone) and tamp it down to form a solid base for the tread stone. Use your level to be certain the tread slopes ever so slightly down in front, so that good drainage is certain. Cut-stone steps should have a slight overhang, or nosing, where the tread meets the riser, so that a shadow forms just under the edge of the step. This is a way of alerting people that a step is there.

The Formula for Step and Tread Measurement

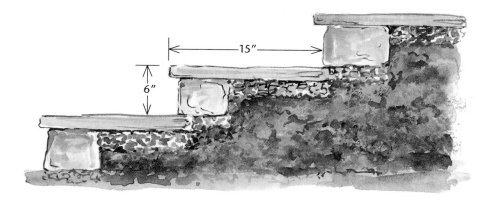

To design steps, use the standard formula: two times the height of the step (the vertical measurement) plus the length of the tread (the horizontal measurement) should equal 27 inches. In this case, 2 x 6 inches + 15 inches = 27 inches. Follow this formula rigidly and no one will trip on your steps.

Brick Paths

Once you have laid a base, laying a brick path is a breeze. There's no need to hire a contractor; this is a job you can do yourself.

Choosing bricks. Bricks are divided into two categories, facing and paving bricks. Make sure you buy paving bricks for outside use, as they are harder and more durable. They are typically two inches thick, four inches wide, and eight inches long, and they cost around forty cents apiece. Because it takes about five bricks to cover a square foot, you can plan on spending around two dollars per square foot. Thus a path fifteen feet long and four feet wide would require sixty square feet of brick — around three hundred bricks — at a cost of about $120.

When choosing the brick for your path, consider the following questions: Will the path be uniformly colored, or do you want slightly different colors brick to brick? Do you want old or new brick? Will you lay the bricks on edge or flat? What pattern will you choose? Will you lay the bricks tight, or will you leave a slight gap? Will you use the same brick set differently as an edging, or will you use metal or wooden edging?

Whatever brick you choose, be sure it has a rough texture so that when people walk on it, their shoes grip the surface well. Some bricks on the market are quite smooth and therefore are a little dangerous for paths.

Choosing a style. The way bricks are arranged in a walkway is called the bond. The more intricate the bond is, the more cutting the bricks will require, so be certain of your ability to cut brick to shape before choosing a pattern. If you are paving a large area such as a terrace or patio, keep the pattern simple; an intricate design is more appropriate for small areas.

If you want to use bricks to edge your path, first decide whether to set them flush with the path or an inch or two above it. In general, protruding bricks are appropriate only to mark the edge between the path and your garden, where they will prevent soil from leaching out onto the path; elsewhere, you want to be sure that people have a flat, safe surface on which to walk. If you want a flat edging, set the bricks flush into the ground, which will hold the interior bricks in place and ensure that the edging won't give way when people walk on it.

Brick Patterns

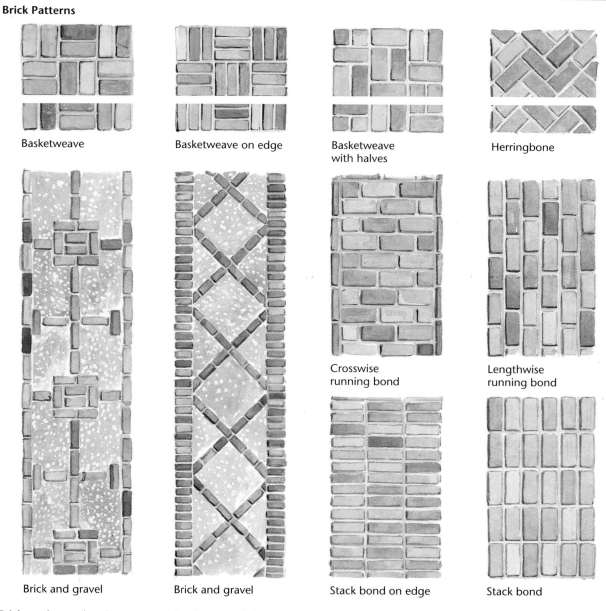

Basketweave

Basketweave on edge

Basketweave
with halves

Herringbone

Brick and gravel

Brick and gravel

Crosswise
running bond

Lengthwise
running bond

Stack bond on edge

Stack bond

Brick can be used on its own or with other materials to create a vast range of patterns. Running bond and stack bond are best for curving paths. Basketweave and herringbone patterns are easy ways to create a straight path.

Laying a Brick Path

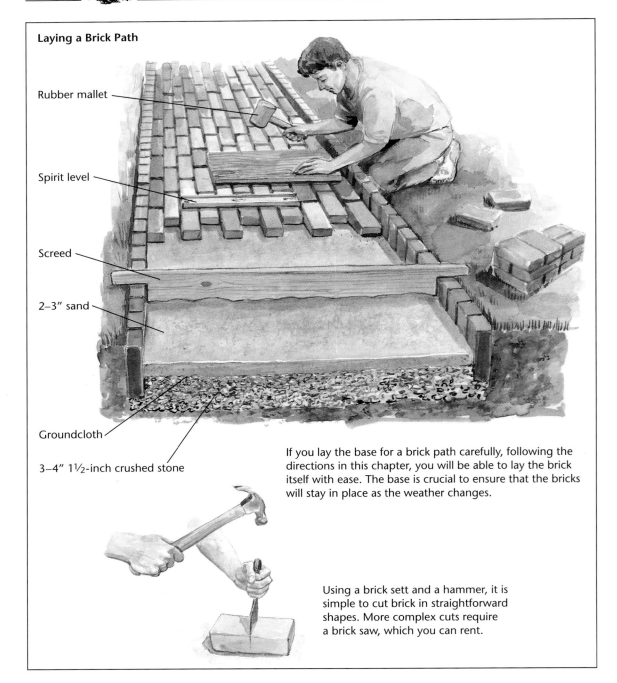

Rubber mallet

Spirit level

Screed

2–3" sand

Groundcloth

3–4" 1½-inch crushed stone

If you lay the base for a brick path carefully, following the directions in this chapter, you will be able to lay the brick itself with ease. The base is crucial to ensure that the bricks will stay in place as the weather changes.

Using a brick sett and a hammer, it is simple to cut brick in straightforward shapes. More complex cuts require a brick saw, which you can rent.

Another option for edging is to lay six-by-six-inch pressure-treated wooden ties, stout metal edging, or granite setts along the length of the path before you lay the bricks. You can then set the bricks into the gap between the ties or stone blocks.

Another factor to consider is the joints between the bricks. Joints with almost no material between them have a tight, refined finish that is most appropriate for a patio, a primary path, or a small garden where formal lines are important. Half-inch-wide joints backfilled with a half-inch of sand look more casual and are best used for sunny pathways or paving through gardens. For naturalized areas of the garden or a narrow path through a meadow, use inch-wide joints.

To give your path a more informal look and create a visual whole with your garden, backfill wide gaps with a loamy sand and set in appropriate plants. If the path is shady, moss makes a good filler; if it is sunny, creeping thyme looks wonderful. You can even remove whole bricks to allow for larger plants such as dianthus, dwarf lady's mantle, or comparable perennials.

Preparing the base. In the northern two thirds of the United States, where heavy, slow-draining soil freezes in the winter, excavate the area for a brick path to a depth of ten to twelve inches. Backfill with six to eight inches of compacted gravel to ensure good drainage, then cover the gravel with two inches of builder's sand and lay the bricks on that. If you have free-draining gravelly or sandy soil, you need to excavate only four to six inches deep and put down two to four inches of sand for the bricks to sit on. The deeper the gravel-and-sand foundation is, the better the drainage will be and the fewer frost heaves your path will suffer.

In areas of the country where the soil rarely freezes, excavate quick-draining soil to a depth of only five or six inches, backfill with three inches of sand, and lay the brick directly on the base. If your soil contains heavy clay, however, build the base so that the surface of the path is at least half an inch above the existing grade. If you set a brick walkway flush with or lower than the grade of the surrounding soil, puddles may form every time it rains, and in the winter those puddles can turn to ice.

Laying the bricks. If you are going to lay a straight brick path, pound stakes into the ground along either side and stretch string between them to establish

Brick set in a running-bond pattern is ideal for making curves and circles.

the edges. Before you lay the brick on sand or stone dust, wet the surface with a hose, tamp it down well, and make sure it is level. Then you are ready to begin laying the bricks. First set out several bricks to be sure that the pattern you have in mind will work. Once you have laid a foot or so of the pattern and feel comfortable with its look, lay the edging bricks along the entire path and then fill in with the pattern.

After you have laid a brick, tap it sharply with a rubber mallet to settle it in. Continually use the spirit level to make sure the bricks align across the path (using the straight edge) and are level (using the bubble).

When you have completed a section, spread a shovelful of sand or stone dust on top of the bricks you've laid, sweep it into the cracks, and sprinkle it with water to settle it. You may have to repeat this process several times before the cracks are full. As with other paving materials, leave a gap of at least half an inch between the top of the bricks and the surface of the backfilling material.

STONE CARPETS

Laying a stone carpet on a bed of sand is even more fun than laying brick, because you need to use your creativity.

Buying the stones. Like cut stone, fieldstones are usually available from masonry suppliers. They come in a variety of colors, thicknesses, and shapes, so it is important to have a clear idea of what colors will look good near your house, what thickness of stone you can handle, and what shapes you like before you explore the options. You will typically pay between $2.50 and $3.50 a square foot, and the stones are usually sold on pallets, which can be delivered to your home for an additional charge.

Laying the stones. The most important part of designing and laying a satisfying stone carpet is making sure that the shapes of the stones speak to one another; that is, a convex area in one stone should fit into a concave area of the next. After you have made the base of the path (see page 37), lay out all your stones on the lawn or on tarps so you can see their shapes. Then start trying out various combinations. Take your time — it is like doing a jigsaw puzzle.

Patterns for Fieldstone Paths

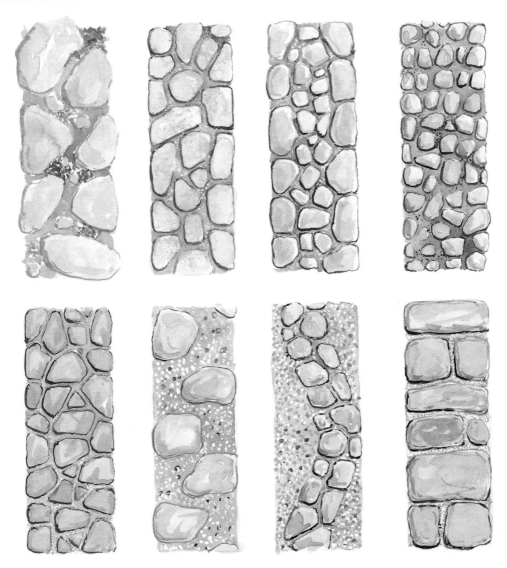

Because fieldstone comes in random shapes, you can create any number of patterns for your path. Fieldstone can also be set into a gravel path to create an interesting look. If you use only small stones, be certain they are set into crusher dust rather than sand, which does not hold them in place as well.

Laying a Stone Carpet

Making a fieldstone walkway is like doing a jigsaw puzzle.
Enjoy the challenge of fitting and shaping pieces to get just the
look you want: tightly laid and formal, or loosely laid and informal.

A four-pound hand sledge hammer and
a mason's chisel will suffice when it
comes to shaping fieldstone. Don't use
a power saw to make your cuts, as they
will look too perfect and stand out from
adjacent stones.

Begin by laying the edging stones to create a pair of clean lines, whether straight or curved. Simply set the stones on top of the sand so you can easily change your mind. Once you've roughly laid five or six feet of edges, fill in between them, arranging the stones to create interesting and complementary shapes. Don't be afraid to shape stones with a mason's hammer to make the shapes work well together.

Once you have a few feet of the path just the way you want it, set the stones permanently into the sand, making sure they are an inch or so above the grade of the adjacent soil so the path will drain well. Tap each one with a rubber mallet to settle it in place. If you are using flat stones, use your spirit level frequently. If you're using fieldstones with a rough surface, you can usually tell whether the stones are level just by looking. When you have permanently laid a section, backfill to within a half-inch of the surface and set a sprinkler on it to settle everything.

If you want to lay a stone carpet in concrete, it is best to have the work done by a professional.

Planning the gaps. You can determine the gaps between individual stones as you lay the carpet, but a general guideline is to set the stones between one half and three quarters of an inch apart. As with cut stone, use large stones on the edges so they don't shift underfoot when stepped on.

GRASS PATHS

In some sites, grass is ideal for making a path: it is quick to establish, easy to design with, and provides a band of color to complement and accent other plantings.

Choosing the materials. There are two ways to establish lawns and lawn-grass paths: by planting grass seed and by laying sod. Though seeding grass is cheaper, there are several advantages to using sod. It gives your path instant coverage. It can be installed anytime during the growing season (though midsummer installations do demand a lot of water) and establishes itself quickly. If you place sod on slopes, it won't wash away, whereas seeded soil often erodes. Since sod is like a carpet, it smothers potential weeds on the soil surface, whereas weeds will sprout if you seed the path.

Sod is sold in strips with root systems that are one half to three quarters of an inch thick and grass that is an inch or two high. The strips are a foot and a half to two feet wide and anywhere from two to five feet long, and even the largest rolls don't weigh more than twenty pounds or thereabouts, so they are easy to carry. These pregrown rolls of mown grass are sold by the square foot, so multiply the length times the width of your path to determine how many square feet you'll need to order for delivery.

If you buy sod directly from the grower, you will probably pay between fifteen and twenty-five cents a square foot. You might pay more if you buy the rolls through a garden center.

Determining the length and width of the path. If you want a path of lawn between sunny perennial beds, consider how wide it should be in relation to the beds. By setting out stakes and strings, you can get a sense of the proportions involved. Naturally, the wider the path, the grander the scale. But if the path is too wide, it will look like a lawn rather than a path, so be careful to keep its width in scale. A good rule of thumb is to make the path no wider than half the width of the widest adjacent bed.

Preparing the soil. Plan ahead: send a soil sample to your nearest testing lab or extension service to learn how to treat it to get a lush lawn.

All weeds, rocks, debris, and existing sod have to be removed from the ground on which you'll be planting the lawn or setting the sod, so use a

Edging a lawn path with stones elegantly solves the problem of grass creeping into adjacent beds.

straight-nosed spade, a sod cutter, or even a round-pointed shovel to dig out the old sod and weeds. If the area is covered with four to six inches of topsoil already, spread lime according to the pH needs of your soil. Then add a starter fertilizer that is high in phosphorus and thus promotes root growth (13-25-12, for example) and till it in to a depth of four inches. Be careful not to use too strong a fertilizer, or it will burn the tender rootlets of the grass. Smooth the surface with an iron rake, roll it with a heavy roller, and then rake over the surface lightly again to smooth out your footprints.

If you are planting seed, simply follow the directions on the seed bag, making sure to keep the path well watered until the grass has established itself. If you are laying sod, prepare the soil well ahead of time, so that when the sod arrives you can lay it immediately. If you leave it even briefly on the pallets on which it is delivered, it will begin to yellow and die. In hot weather, it should be laid within twelve hours of being harvested at the sod farm; in cool weather, thirty-six hours is the maximum.

Laying the sod. Where you lay the first strip of sod determines where every other piece goes, so choose your starting point carefully. If the path runs along an existing border, stretch string tightly between four stakes to outline the path. Begin laying sod at one end and work toward the other. If you're working on a slope, lay the sod lengthwise across the slope to prevent erosion. Be careful when you roll out each sod; it does tear. Just before you begin, water the area lightly so the soil does not pull moisture from already stressed rootlets. Though it is important to keep the sods moist, don't water deeply until the whole job is done, or you'll be working in a mudbath.

Once you have the first sod in place, set a small board or piece of plywood atop it to take your weight as you set the next piece. This prevents your knees from making indentations as you work down the path. Be sure that each piece fits snugly against the adjoining ones along the sides and at the ends, for it is at the outer edges that the sods can dry out. Also, when you start the second row, be sure to alternate the joints, just as you would when laying brick. That is, the first sod at the side of the path should be full length, the sod that begins the next row should be half a length, the next one full, the next one half, and so on. Cut sods with a serrated kitchen knife or a very sharp straight-nosed spade.

Finishing the job. Once you have laid all the sods, go over the whole path with a roller to press the undersides of the sods into contact with the soil and get rid of any air pockets. If you find gaps between sods, sprinkle a mixture of moistened peat moss and topsoil into them. The grass will fill in the space quickly. Then set up an oscillating sprinkler and water the path thoroughly. While the grass is taking root, water as needed — at least every other day (or even daily if the weather is hot and dry) — keeping an eye on the edges of the sods, which dry out first. Keep up this watering schedule for two or three weeks.

Laying a Sod Path

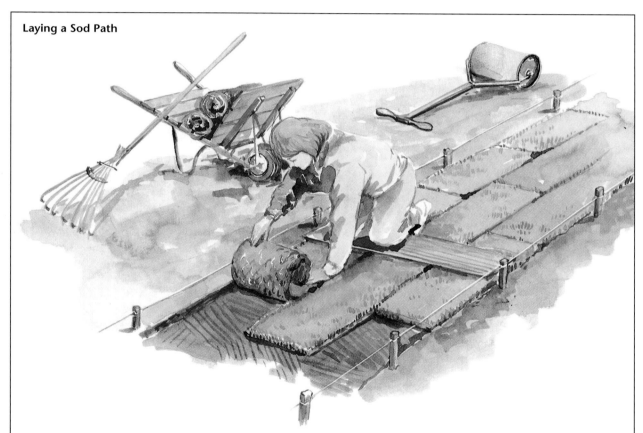

Laying sod is simple and satisfying. Once you have prepared the base, it is simply a matter of rolling out a green carpet. Then you need to water, water, water. If you use a board to kneel on as you lay the sod, you won't create depressions in the grass and its base.

STEPPING-STONE PATHS

When you think of stepping stones, you probably think of flat fieldstones, but stepping stones are also made of other materials. You can buy square, rectangular, or circular pavers of various sizes made from precast concrete, or geometric cut stones, also in various sizes. It is best not to use wooden rounds as stepping stones, as they are very slippery when wet and they break down in only a few years and have to be replaced.

Fieldstones that are slightly convex drain readily and provide a slightly rounded shape that rises to accept the foot; they should have some texture and roughness to ensure a good grip. Concrete pavers are lighter in color and tend to look a bit foreign unless they are used near a stucco home, and cut stones are most appropriately laid in straight lines, since they are geometric. All of these materials are best laid on the standard base described on page 37, but if the soil drains well, you can set them directly into it. Plan on laying the paths yourself.

Laying the stones. The best way to determine where to set stepping stones is to rake the area where the path will be and then walk along it, moving at a comfortable pace. The center of each stone should go where your foot falls with each step. Of course, your pace isn't the same as everyone else's, but if you will use the path most frequently, it makes sense to set the stones where you will step on them.

The distance between the individual stones determines the pace at which people move. If you want visitors to slow down to look at plants, views, or garden sculpture, leave a gap no greater than six inches between the stones. If you want to encourage people to move along the path more quickly, leave gaps of ten to twelve inches.

When setting stepping stones into your lawn, first decide whether to lay them flush with the grass so you can run the lawn mower right over them or to lay them an inch or so above the surrounding grade, creating a stronger visual contrast but necessitating hand-trimming. In a cultivated garden, stones are usually set about an inch above ground level. This creates shadows around the edges, and moss or other groundcovers can creep up to the stones and perhaps even cover them a little.

Before setting any stones permanently into the ground, lay them all out where they will go, using the larger stones at the beginning or end of the path. When

Stepping-Stone Patterns

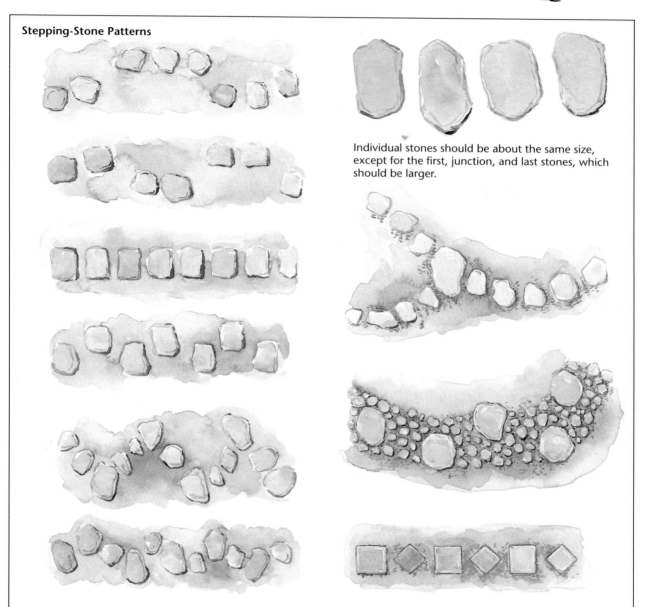

Individual stones should be about the same size, except for the first, junction, and last stones, which should be larger.

Fieldstones used as stepping stones can be laid in any number of ways, but they always look best in a curving, meandering path. Cut stones look better in a straight line and are typically used this way in Japanese-style gardens. Stepping stones can also be combined with river rocks and gravel, or they can be set directly in the lawn.

Ground-hugging plants will quickly fill in the gaps between stepping stones, making the path an integral part of the garden. Some will also release wonderful fragrance when stepped on.

positioning smaller stones, pay attention to their shapes and try to create relationships between them. In general, it is best to lay the length of the stepping stones across the path rather than parallel to its direction.

Setting the stones. Once you have laid out the whole path, with all the stones oriented the way you want them, you are ready to set them. Using a trowel or a straight-nosed spade, mark the outline of the first stone on the path and then lift it and place it to the side in the position in which it will lie; in that way you won't forget how to set it. Excavate the soil below where the step will go to a depth of six to eight inches, backfill with crushed gravel, and then set the stone on top of its base. Tap it into place with a rubber mallet and backfill around the edges with more crushed gravel.

You can lay stepping stones directly on the earth or lawn if they are thick and heavy enough to stay in place when stepped on. However, if you live where winters get cold, you will find that frost heaves the stones around. If this is a problem in your area, make a standard base as described on page 37 and lay the stepping stones on top of it, filling around them with the soil you remove.

CRUSHED STONE OR GRAVEL PATHS

Because making these paths does not call for a lot of experience, you will probably want to lay them yourself if you wish to save money. Otherwise, hire someone to do the work under your direction.

Choosing the right material. Crushed gravel, with particles no larger than $1/4$ inch square, and the slightly coarser crushed stone have several advantages as paving materials. Crushed gravel that comes from your area blends particularly well with your garden, as it picks up the color and texture of any rocks or boulders on your property and accents plant colors. Over time, the tiny angular pieces of fine-textured crushed stone settle into the gravel foundation, forming a path that stays put and looks natural. These materials also crunch underfoot, adding the pleasing dimension of sound to your garden and alerting you to the path itself.

Although many kinds of gravel and crushed stone are appropriate, be cautious about using white or light gravels or marble chips. These colors contrast so

*Perennials planted beside a meandering gravel path soften its edges and link it
visually with the surrounding garden.*

strongly with green plants and brown soil that they jar the eye, disturbing the feeling of peacefulness you want in a garden.

Gravel and crushed stone are among the least expensive paving materials. Order them by the cubic yard from a sand-and-gravel supplier and have them delivered. To get the correct figure, multiply the length of your proposed path by the width by the depth (two to three inches) and divide by twenty-seven.

Laying gravel or crushed stone. When walking on a gravel path, you want to feel that the ground is solid underfoot. With that in mind, lay your path on a three- to four-inch base of coarser gravel or crushed stone to assure good drainage. If your path will be made of crushed stone and you are laying it in top-soil, excavate a trench the length of the path to a depth of eight to ten inches. For damp or slow-draining soil, lay an inch or two of $1\frac{1}{2}$-inch crushed stone, then place a 4-inch perforated PVC drainpipe along the path (with the holes down) to carry excess water off the downhill side. Cap the highest end of the pipe to prevent soil from clogging it, and place a grate at the lowest end to prevent small animals from crawling up. Then lay four inches of $1\frac{1}{2}$-inch crushed stone on top of the pipe.

Before you put down the finer layer of gravel that will form the path, lay woven black plastic groundcloth on top of the base. This will keep the top finer layer from leaching into the coarser crushed stone below causing the drainpipe to clog.

Once the cloth is down, spread two inches of screened gravel on top of it. Water this layer and tamp it down, and then place one inch of finely crushed stone on top to complete the path. The final path should be about one inch below the grade of the surrounding surface so the gravel doesn't migrate onto the lawn or into adjoining beds as people walk along. Because the gravel, the cloth, and the crushed stone base are all porous, there is little chance that water will accumulate on the path.

If your soil drains freely, use a simpler approach. Excavate to a depth of five inches, lay in four inches of screened gravel, wet, tamp, and then lay down the one-inch top dressing and tamp it down.

Edgings for Gravel Paths

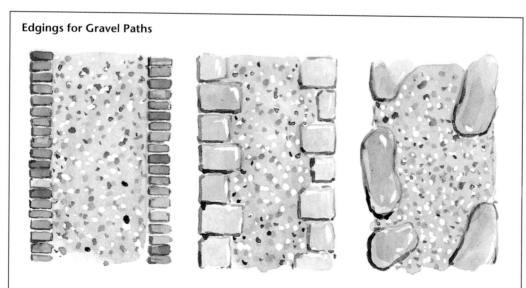

Plants in adjacent beds or the lawn can serve as edging for crushed gravel paths. Brick, cut stone, or fieldstone are also appropriate.

PINE-NEEDLE, BARK-MULCH, AND EARTH PATHS

Hire someone to do the hard work of preparing the base for the path, and then you can have the fun of laying the surface.

Pine-needle paths. If the soil where you want to create a pine-needle path is solid and free-draining, there is no need to do any preparation. Simply rake the surface and spread pine or spruce needles from a nearby woods onto your path.

If you think the soil will turn muddy when it rains, excavate to a depth of eight inches and lay down five inches of gravel. Put two inches of bark mulch on top of that, and then lay down one to two inches of pine needles. The bark mulch will provide the springiness you associate with pine needles in a forest, and it retains moisture, thereby helping to keep the needles flexible. Annual replacement may be necessary, but when the needles do break down and decompose, another organic substance — the bark mulch — is exposed, so the illusion of the forest floor is kept relatively intact.

To get the pine needles for your path, rake them from roadsides or driveways in late September, when they fall naturally from white pines. In North Carolina and Georgia, longleaf or slash pine needles are so plentiful that they are baled for sale.

Bark-mulch paths. Bark mulch is another good choice for informal, natural-looking paths. If there are lumber mills in your area, you can buy large amounts of bark mulch from them at low cost. In southern Vermont, for example, a mill will load a pickup truck for between $35 and $50, depending on the size of the truck's bed (most hold about three cubic yards). In contrast, bagged mulch from a garden center usually costs about three or four dollars a bag, and each bag holds only two to three cubic feet. If you live where there are no mills, try to buy bulk mulch from landscaping firms or agricultural co-ops.

To lay a bark-mulch path on heavy or slow-draining soil, excavate a six- to eight-inch-deep trench, backfill it with four inches of coarse gravel or crushed stone, and lay the mulch on top. If you don't use gravel, the soil under a three- or four-inch layer of bark mulch can become muddy.

If the soil drains freely, just dig a three- or four-inch-deep trench and fill it with bark mulch. An alternative is to spread the bark mulch directly onto the soil, creating a four-inch-high raised path. When the mulch breaks down in a

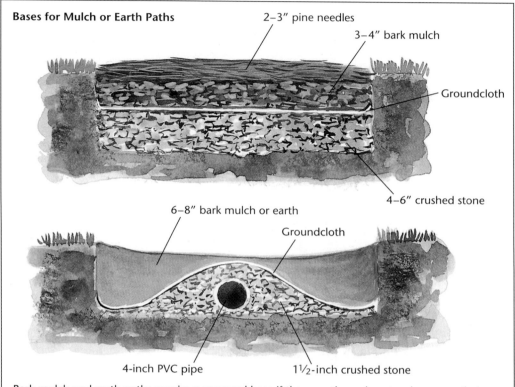

Bases for Mulch or Earth Paths

2–3″ pine needles

3–4″ bark mulch

Groundcloth

4–6″ crushed stone

6–8″ bark mulch or earth

Groundcloth

4-inch PVC pipe

1½-inch crushed stone

Bark-mulch and earth paths require a prepared base if they run through wet or low areas that are slow to drain. If your soil drains freely, you can make an earth path simply by raking leaves and other detritus from its surface. The key to a bark-mulch path is to lay down just enough mulch to cover the forest floor and achieve the springiness you associate with natural woodland.

year or two, you can simply fork the decomposed material into the soil in adjoining beds and replace it with fresh bark mulch.

Earth paths. Trodden earth paths underpin the natural feeling of a garden and often almost make themselves: paths from the pond up to the barn or through the woods to a neighbor's house seem to appear out of nowhere. To keep the drainage good and to prevent mud, spread a wheelbarrow load of crushed gravel every six feet on ground that has been raked free of debris. Rake the gravel to a uniform thickness and then fork or rototill it into the soil.

II.

Using Paths to Design Your Garden

CHAPTER 4
STARTING FROM SCRATCH

No matter how big your property is and no matter where you want to put your garden, paths are a good way to start the design. Through their materials and direction, they link your house with the surrounding land, helping to create a coherent harmony. Because the house is the visual center of the garden, you can use its style and materials — whether Pennsylvania stone, California redwood, New England clapboard, Florida stucco, or Georgia brick — to determine the style of both your paths and your garden. Look at the doors of your house for clues as to where to put the primary walkways; once you have paths reaching out into the landscape, you will be able to see where you might put secondary and tertiary paths, and thus garden areas.

If you have a formal and traditional home, you will want to have rather formal gardens and paths near it: for example, a straight path of cut stone or brick to the front door, with symmetrically planted beds on either side. If your house

The transformation of lawn into this area of the author's garden began with the brick path, which follows a straight line between the apple tree in the background and the front door of the house. The addition of two side paths created a square garden with four quadrants and suggested the placement of the garden ornament.

is more informal, a curving stone carpet might look right, with asymmetrical plantings and a loose, free-flowing feel to the garden.

ENTRANCE GARDENS

The dimensions of your home can help you determine the proportions of the gardens in general and the front garden in particular. One way to begin is to measure the height of the front wall of your house and take that as the distance from the house to the far edge of the garden. For instance, if the front wall of the house is twenty feet high, you could put a fence or a stone wall twenty feet out from the corners of the house and across the full width of the front, leaving a gate in the center for a path in from the sidewalk. The resulting enclosure is where you will plant your entrance garden.

Similarly, you can use the width of the front door and any associated trim (or of a porch or portico over the door) to determine the width of the main path through the entrance garden. If you lay a narrower secondary path parallel to the house, across the entrance garden, and around the corner, it will take visitors to gardens running along the side of the house and on into the backyard.

Once you have come up with a clear structure like this, you can lay your paths and begin to plant, keeping to the mood and style appropriate for the house. If it's a country house and the entrance faces south, you might consider a patterned herb garden like the ones often planted in front of Williamsburg colonials, with a picket fence twenty to thirty feet out and brick paths and boxwood edging for the beds. If you live in a more formal home, you might divide the entrance garden into symmetrical square or rectangular beds and plant a small ornamental tree surrounded by a ground cover in the center of each one.

A relaxed suburban home calls for yet another approach. Say you have a long lawn that slopes down to a sidewalk. One option is to build a stone retaining wall to create a flat area about twenty feet away from the house. Then you might lay a cut-stone path from the sidewalk to the front door, with a set of steps through the wall to a broad stone landing on the flat area. To make the entrance even more welcoming, plant a pair of small ornamental trees on either side of the steps and underplant them with shade-tolerant shrubs, perennials, and bulbs, creating an appealing environment of movement, light, and color.

SIDE GARDENS

Most beginning gardeners regard the areas along the sides of the house as utilitarian passageways leading to the back of the house or the garage. By using a little imagination and building secondary paths down their typically long and shady lengths, however, you can turn these forgotten parts of the landscape into richly planted gardens.

Of course, a path from the garage door to the kitchen door must be practical and predictable, so you can walk with bags of groceries and not have to look where you are putting your feet. Cut stones laid tightly together might be appropriate. However, a walk that runs from the front to the back of the house, with the garage

A lawn path between two gardens will pull them together visually if it is of uniform width, giving visitors the feeling that they are walking through a single garden rather than two separate ones.

Imagine this as a model for a garden between your house and the fence, wall, or hedge separating your property from your neighbor's. The brick path leads people from the front to the back of your home, providing visual variety along the way.

at one side, might be made of stepping stones. Each of these paths can act as the spine of a long, narrow shade garden planted with whatever is suitable for your climate and taste and the style of your house. You might put in tall trees or shade-tolerant shrubs beside the path and underplant them with evergreen shrubs, ferns, and bulbs, using groundcovers to creep around the stepping stones. Or, if you live somewhere warm and sunny, you might make a low-growing garden of succulents and drought-tolerant herbs, with a few shrubs or cacti as focal points.

If you link these two side paths with the primary path along the front, you create two junctions, one on the right and one on the left side of your home.

This side garden near the house follows the lines of the structure. In this case, the center of the path lines up with the trimwork between the two windows, and the outer hedge, in line with the path, provides a background for the flower bed. The whole property is in harmony.

Junctions are frequently good places for trees, which in turn are good places for underplantings of shrubs, perennials, and groundcovers.

The walls of the house or garage might support trelliswork on which to grow shade-tolerant vines such as climbing hydrangea or clematis. Plant the gaps between the stepping stones with ground-hugging plants that won't mind being stepped on. If there is a turn in the path, place a boulder, a small shrub, or a tree in the curve. If one of the paths leads away from a fence, mark the beginning with a gate and place potted plants beside it. Use your imagination, and let the structure of the buildings and paths suggest ideas.

A simple stone path laid out in straight lines can link a bit of woodland with a lot of lawn, especially if it serves as an edging for a varied garden that flows seamlessly into the trees.

PATIOS AND TERRACES

When a path along the side of the house reaches the back, it's a good idea to turn it toward a terrace or patio outside the back door. This gives the side path or paths a clear destination, and the patio or terrace serves as a visual center, from which another path might lead out to a garden ornament, a vegetable garden, or a grove of trees.

Patios are generally made of stone or brick and are rectangular or semicircular; that is, their style and shape are related to those of the adjacent house. A patio or terrace provides a number of places for plants and garden ornaments. If it gets too hot in the sun, you can provide shade by planting trees at the corners or where the path joins it. A perennial bed or a fragrance garden looks nice beside the stone or brick, or, if you're looking for a garden that needs little maintenance, you can put in an evergreen or peony hedge along the sides. Trees, shrubs, or a small water feature such as a bubbler or a little fountain work well at the corners of a patio. The surface itself is a perfect place to display planted terra-cotta pots. You can even take up some of the stones or bricks and plant thyme or any perennial that will thrive in spite of being walked on.

BACK GARDENS

One interesting design might be to continue the two paths that run along the sides of the house out to the back garden and on to the far corners of your property. There they can turn toward a gazebo, a sitting area, or even a little orchard or a vegetable garden with a bench in it. If you plant both sides of these paths with shrubs and trees, you will walk through a woodsy tunnel to your destination. Gaps in the planting will afford a view now and again into the center of your back lawn.

Another option is to bisect the length of your backyard with a fence or a hedge that runs parallel to the back of your house. Then run a path down the middle from your terrace or patio. If your lawn is, say, sixty feet long, you could divide it into two thirty-foot halves by planting a hedge from one side to the other, with a simple arbor or gate in the middle, in line with the center of your terrace or your back door. When guests follow the primary path of grass or gravel past flower beds to the arbor, they are invited to explore all the way to the back of your property.

Gates and entrances also suggest places for plants. If your home is urban and formal, a symmetrical pair of crab-apple trees or Bradford pears on either side of the gate, with a clematis growing up each gatepost, would be appropriate. If your home is more rustic, you might consider an arbor for a climbing rose over the gateway. Arbors are also good places to put garden furniture, especially if you plant vines to run up the supports. The sides and back of these structures might be places for fragrant perennials, small shrubs, or potted plants — or any number of other design ideas.

Even in a small patch of woodland, a narrow path of earth made by raking away the leaves serves as an invitation to explore. Planting along the edges of the path will add further interest to the walk.

Planning a Unified Design

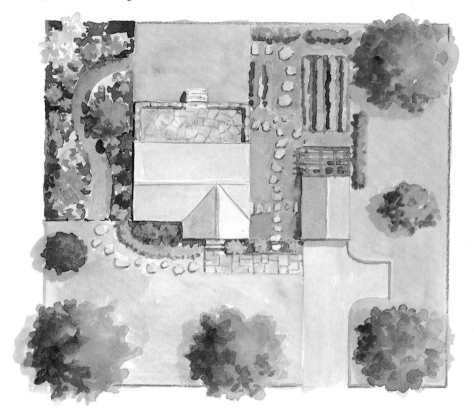

By combining paths around your home with fences, trees, shrubs, and new beds, you can create entrance, side, and back gardens that use the space in completely new ways.

If the far back of your property consists of a small oak and pine woods (as you often find in Georgia), a bit of desert (as in Arizona), or a mixed hardwood copse (as in the Midwest), you should consider running a simple bark-mulch or gravel path through the indigenous plants. No matter what the specifics are, use your paths to link all the elements of your property, from the cultivated to the uncultivated. The more variety you can offer, the more stimulating your garden becomes.

Chapter 5
Pulling an Existing Garden Together

Paths and the edges of the beds that they establish are central to the structure of a coherent garden. In order for a garden to seem unified, all its lines, whether established by flower beds, the driveway, the patio, the driplines of trees, or a primary path leading from the back door, need to relate to one another within an overarching concept. Invariably, this means simplifying the shapes of existing beds and establishing new relationships between old and new ones.

For example, you might buy a house where there are already two free-form flower beds on the back lawn, a vegetable garden in a corner, and the beginnings of an herb garden by the patio, with a large section of lawn in the middle. Each of these gardens may be well designed, but if their lines do not relate to one another, your property will look incoherent. Paths can be very helpful in creating relationships between these disparate elements. But first it is important to understand two design elements: positive and negative space.

Here the logical curve of the foundation bed around a crab apple is echoed by the curve of the shrub plantings beyond it. The negative space of the lawn path links the two gardens together.

DESIGN ELEMENTS TO CONSIDER

Positive space is an area to which the eye is drawn because something is happening there, whereas negative space is an area that the eye passes over quickly. Around a house, flower beds and other gardens are positive spaces; the lawn that surrounds them is negative space. In order to achieve a coherent look, you must create a relationship between all these spaces.

To determine what relationships already exist among your individual garden spaces, go outside and look at the shapes of the beds. Does the shape of one bed echo that of another close by? Do the edges of adjacent beds curve in the same way or in different ways? If your beds have straight lines, are they parallel to each another, or do they go off at different angles?

Now look at the shape of the lawn — that is, the negative space — by looking down from an upstairs window, or even from a ladder leaning against the house. Imagine the lawn as a large piece of green paper with spaces cut out where your beds are. Do you see any pattern in the resulting shape of the lawn? Is the amount of lawn in proportion to the sizes of the beds? Are your beds little islands in a sea of grass, or can you barely see the grass between the beds?

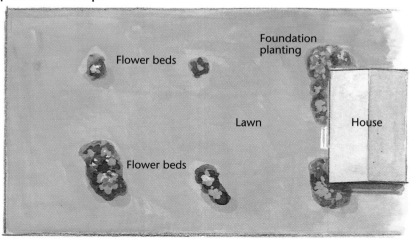

Poor Spatial Relationships

Positive space (flower beds, the house, terraces, and so on) must be in proportion to negative space (the lawn). In this case, the negative space overwhelms the positive space so that the four tiny beds and the foundation planting have no relationship to one another.

Well-Designed Formal Spatial Relationships

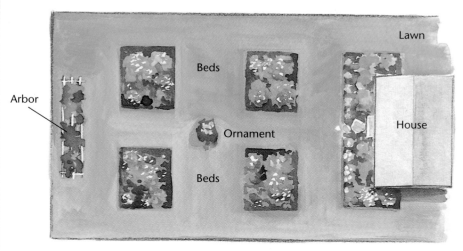

Here the positive and negative spaces are in proportion, the lines are related, and the garden pattern is pleasing.

Well-Designed Informal Spatial Relationships

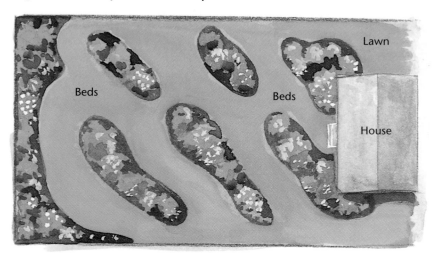

Curves can also be used to create a pleasing relationship between positive and negative space. In this instance, all the curving lines relate to one another while the roughly uniform spaces between the beds act as paths.

The straight lines of this gravel path through the garden relate it to the straight lines of the house and the fieldstone path, but the choice of paving material and the informal plantings soften the edges to create a relaxed feeling.

The next step is to ask "Why is that there?" of everything in the garden, including the shapes of the beds. Take a close look at the shapes of beds, paths, and patios near your house. You might even want to make simple scaled drawings, outlining the house and the edges of adjacent beds. Ask yourself why those lines move as they do. Are there curves for the sake of curving, or do the curves flow logically around trees, shrubs, boulders, or ornaments? There is nothing worse in a garden than a curve that cannot be justified.

In fact, we Americans seem to have an innate distrust of straight lines in the garden. Maybe we think they are too formal, too snobbish — related, perhaps,

To achieve a unified look, take up some of the sod between several small beds in the lawn and make one or two big beds. A path can then link the beds with each other, with the house, or with an outbuilding at the back of the property.

to the carefully geometric shapes of some European gardens. In general, we are much more comfortable with democratic curves, which we often say "soften the edges." But the fact is that both straight and curving edges are appropriate, and each has its place in the garden. Keep an open mind about this, and use the lines and proportions of the house to generate the shapes and proportions of nearby garden elements such as terraces, patios, planting beds, panels of lawn, and the entrance garden. As you move farther and farther away from the house, you can let go of straight lines and sharp angles and gradually introduce curves, which reflect the more casual, less contrived forms of nature. The geometric lines of a shed near the tree line might tie the whole together.

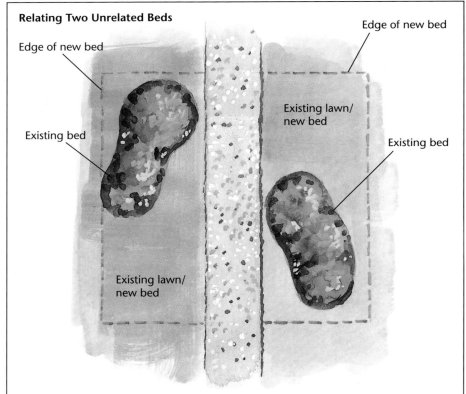

Relating Two Unrelated Beds

Edge of new bed

Edge of new bed

Existing bed

Existing lawn/ new bed

Existing bed

Existing lawn/ new bed

Beds remain unrelated when their edges don't create a meaningful shape in the lawn between them. To bring them together, make them into two large rectangular beds bisected by a straight path of either gravel or lawn.

USING PATHS TO CREATE COHERENCE

Suppose the two free-form beds in the lawn of your new house are within six or eight feet of each another, but the shape of the lawn between them does nothing to relate them visually. Could you make a uniformly shaped rectangular or curving path of grass between them to act as a link? If so, would the new, uniform shape of the path have any implications for how you might change the shapes of the two beds?

To help you decide what would look best, consider the edges of your other beds to see if any of them have satisfying shapes or forms that you might repeat in the free-form beds. Does the herb garden have broadly curving edges? Can

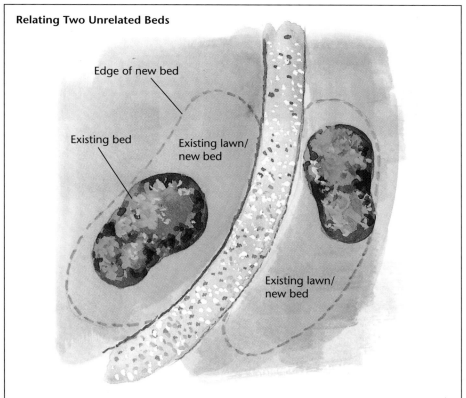

Relating Two Unrelated Beds

Edge of new bed

Existing bed

Existing lawn/
new bed

Existing lawn/
new bed

Unrelated beds can also be brought into a relationship with curves. The key to doing this successfully is to make the path between the two new beds uniformly wide, creating a visual constant.

The height of the gardens beside a path can affect how it looks in the landscape. Here the taller plants on the right hide the curve in the path, lending mystery to the destination; those on the left give balance to the garden as a whole.

you use the sight line created by a set of steps on the terrace to determine how the path between the free-form beds might go? Does the rectangular shape of the terrace suggest that you should remake the beds in a rectangular shape, with a rectangular path between them?

In other words, don't look at your beds as separate units. Try to see their shapes in relation to all other parts of your garden. Nearly every straight line in my own one-and-a-half-acre garden, for example, is either parallel or perpendicular to the south side of the house.

Once you see where the path should go and how to reshape the beds, create the new shapes by cutting out sod as necessary. Then rototill lots of compost into the new areas of the beds so that you can plant out to the edges. If any of the existing plants need transplanting or dividing, you can use them to fill in the new space.

You will also want to consider what new plants you would like to introduce. For instance, if you have combined two free-form beds into one by running a path through them, you might plant a shrub at each end of the path to tie the whole together. Or you might put trees beside the path and make a shade garden. If you already have a rectangular bed with a low hedge elsewhere in the garden, you might plant a similar hedge around the edges of this new bed or along either side of the path.

Are there any shrubs near the house that might be repeated in your new garden to create a new relationship? Does the path suggest where they should go? Do you want to broaden the path in the middle and place a sundial or a birdbath on a pedestal? If so, what will you plant around the base of the pedestal? Would it be a good idea to set the same plant along the edges of the path?

Once you have decided how to tie your two free-form beds together into a visual whole with a path, you can begin to look at your other beds with an eye to forming relationships with this new garden. Good ideas ripple out to create other good ideas.

HOW TO DEAL WITH CURVES

The biggest problem with curving bed edges is to make them look natural and logical. Most of the curves in my garden, for instance, follow the dripline of trees — that is, the tips of the branches — so they seem logical and relate to one another. I turn the area between the dripline and the tree trunks into beds; the dripline itself is edged lawn.

Another way to create a logically curving bed around a tree is to duplicate what I did with a mature apple tree growing in my lawn. Several unrelated beds had already been established outside the dripline of the apples, some of them twenty feet away and others closer. I tied a string long enough to reach ten feet beyond the dripline in a big loose loop around the tree's trunk, then walked in

This meandering brick path curves naturally around large shrubs and trees, leading visitors on an interesting tour.

a circle around the trunk, setting stakes in the ground every eight feet or so. Then I took up all the lawn outside this big circle to create a single new edge to what had been the unrelated beds surrounding the tree. I planted the open ground between the beds with divisions of plants already in them. The beds immediately came into relationship with each other, and the apple tree now sits proudly in the center of a circle of lawn.

If you already have beds with curving edges and you want to leave them in place, plant a shrub or tree just where the bed curves to make the curve look like it belongs there. Often beginning gardeners establish a curved perennial bed that bulges out from the front two corners of the house. If you plant shrubs just at the corners, within the beds, the curve will appear much more logical.

What is the moral of this tale? Whenever possible, simplify shapes so as to keep both the positive and the negative spaces uncluttered by extraneous wiggles and curves. As a bonus, this practice invariably makes maintenance, especially lawn mowing, easier.

CHAPTER 6
ALTERNATIVES TO FOUNDATION PLANTING

Foundation planting is what we plant along the foundation of a house. The reason for it is that we have remained tenaciously loyal to a pattern established about a hundred years ago, when houses were built on exposed four- or five-foot-high foundations. We don't plant yews, rhododendrons, junipers, and azaleas in front of our houses because we like to; we do it because we don't know what else to do. We're in a rut. Fortunately, the concept of the path can help us find new ways to plant around our houses, so we create exciting gardens that we can walk into and enjoy.

The typical route we Americans lay out for our guests is this: park the car, walk to the front door, go into the house, go out the back door, sit on the patio, and perhaps take a walk around the backyard. What happens to all that space at the front of the house? Only passersby pay much attention to that area. And what about the land along the sides of the house? That's where we store the

A gravel path through a garden of trees, shrubs, and perennials right next to the house makes a satisfying alternative to foundation planting. In this case, a spare modern home is enhanced by a Japanese-style garden.

By running a path through a thickly planted garden between the sidewalk and the front of the house, you give passersby a glimpse of your home but still maintain your privacy. The path to the front door is broad and inviting, while the narrower cut-stone path at the side encourages exploration.

canoe or the garbage cans. We need to reclaim what is now semipublic space, particularly at the front of our homes, and make it private or at least semiprivate space.

But in doing so, we must develop a way to draw people into our gardens. The best way to do that is to make a path that invites people to follow an itinerary around our homes. In this way, the house really does become the center of the garden. Once we let go of the time-worn notion of the narrow foundation planting along the front of the house, once we begin to see the value of walking *through* front and side gardens, we begin to open up an entirely new way of gardening. The range of plants we can use becomes vast. Logical places for plants

This gravel path across the front of an informal home clearly invites visitors to turn the corner to see the side and back gardens. The gardens on both sides are planted with colorful perennials and shrubs.

and garden ornaments and fences and hedges and gates and potted plants and annuals and perennials and shrubs and trees and sitting areas start to appear. And it is the path that leads people through all these new elements, linking them together in a harmonious whole.

THE PATH FROM THE SIDEWALK TO THE FRONT DOOR

In most American homes, the primary path in front of the house runs either from the garage past the foundation plantings to the front door or from the sidewalk across the lawn and between foundation plantings to the front door.

Let's look at the path from the sidewalk first. Consider planting a combination of shrubs and perennials in three-foot-wide beds on either side of the path so that when you walk along it, there are all kinds of wonderful plants to look at, touch, and smell. If the path comes up a slight slope, add steps along the way to create a new level of interest.

You might want to combine the plantings beside the path with a new garden that extends ten or fifteen feet from the foundation, replacing some of the lawn. Plant shrubs, perennials, or ornamental grasses in this wide bed, and perhaps add a small sitting area between the taller plants and the house. In this way you can actually be within the garden as well as admire it from the windows at the front of your home.

To provide more privacy, consider planting five- or six-foot-high shrubs, grasses, or a hedge along the sidewalk or several feet in from it and, if you live in a snowless area, along the edge of your driveway. In a front garden I saw in Cambridge, Massachusetts, the owner had put up a solid but decorative wooden fence beside the sidewalk and then made a garden of the entire fifty-foot space between the fence and the house. To give passersby a brief view into the garden, she installed an openwork wrought-iron gate in the fence.

If we think in new ways and are willing to give up the notion of foundation planting, then we can use the edges of the driveway, the sidewalk, and the path from the sidewalk to the front door as logical places along which to plant perennials and shrubs and even trees. These plantings don't need to be complex. A shady path from the sidewalk to the front door can be edged with something as simple as widely spaced boxwoods underplanted with *Vinca minor* 'Bowles', in the Northeast, or with a mix of *Stachys byzantina,* lavender, armeria, penstemon, and sedum, in the Southwest. The point is to see the path as the spine of a bed.

THE PATH FROM THE DRIVEWAY OR GARAGE TO THE FRONT DOOR

Most often this path is four or five feet away from the foundation, and the space between its inner edge and the house is planted with the usual shrubs and a few perennials. To improve on this traditional approach, consider taking up three feet of lawn on the *outside* of the path and planting that in perennials and shrubs as

A broad brick path to the front door can serve as the spine for a garden in light shade. Here the garden extends well out from the front of the house, providing a richly varied alternative to the standard foundation planting.

well, so that people walk through a garden. There is no better place than this path to provide fragrance and color, for both play a role in welcoming you and your guests.

Don't let that path just stop halfway across the front of the house, either. Make a broad landing just outside the front door and then continue the path until you get well past the corner. That's when you get to the true no man's land — the side garden, where, not knowing what else to do, we plant yews, rhododendrons, junipers, and a few annuals by way of foundation planting. Here's an alternative.

THE SIDE GARDEN

One way to approach the side garden is to run a solid wooden fence (or a picket or split-rail fence) with a gate in it from the corner of the house to the edge of your property. The path can either run across the front to the gate and then down the side or start at the gate. If you plant shrubs and perennials on either side of the fence, you might even screen the back garden from the view of anyone in the front and gain a great deal of privacy.

 The path running down the side of the house can be made of brick, stepping stones, cut stones laid six to nine inches apart, or, if you live in the country, bark mulch or pine needles. To increase your privacy, set up a fence or plant trees, large shrubs, or a dense evergreen or deciduous hedge along your property line, dividing your place visually from your neighbors'. This might give you the opportunity to add a paved sitting area with a bench or a chair or two, or it might provide the perfect site for a garden sculpture.

 Once you have established the structure of the side garden with a hedge, a path, a gate, and perhaps a sitting area, you can begin to plant the garden. If the area is hot and dry, consider planting trees for shade, or plant perennials and shrubs that like sunny conditions. If you live in the Southwest, for example, you might consider laying a gravel walkway through plantings of Mexican evening primrose, red yucca, purple lantana, indigo bush, blackfoot daisies, and penstemons — a combination I saw in a side garden near Phoenix, Arizona.

 Another possibility is to choose one large plant with dramatic foliage, such as the red-leaved barberry *(Berberis thunbergii atropurpurea),* a sun-lover. Place three of them at intervals along both sides of the path to add internal structure to the side garden. This gives you the opportunity to pick perennials that will complement the foliage of your chosen shrub. In this case, you might highlight the dark red leaves of the barberries with *Hypericum prolificum,* which has yellow flowers and light green leaves; *Alchemilla mollis,* which has long-lasting chartreuse flowers; or any of the catmints with lavender-blue flowers.

 Whatever you decide to do with the garden on the far side of the house, it will give you all kinds of clues as to how to treat the side garden between the house and the garage. You might use the same paving material, the same kind of trees, and perhaps the same shrubs and groundcovers. Or you might underplant the same trees with different shrubs and perennials. Of course, the two side gar-

The area between a driveway and the side of the house can be a good place for a stone carpet planted with perennials and evergreens. In this garden in the Southwest, the color of the adobe suggested suitable color schemes for the garden.

dens should not be drastically different from each other, because you want to create visual harmony throughout your property.

I know of a house in California completely surrounded by a woodland garden. A stepping-stone path snakes from the driveway and from the path to the front door across the front garden and down the side garden, where it flows around a small pool. The stepping stones then broaden into a sitting area under

The curving brick path that leads to this side door broadens to provide two generous sitting areas. Shrubs and fencing provide privacy for these inviting places in the shade.

an apple tree before turning back into a path that runs through the other side garden and out to the other side of the driveway. There is no lawn anywhere. The owners are fanatical gardeners, and the place is beautifully designed. You may not want to take on such a big project, but this is a fine example of how letting go of the idea of foundation planting can help us create whole new worlds of possibilities for our gardens.

THE BACK GARDEN

Once you understand how to put together the side gardens and the paths through them, the back garden practically creates itself. The design for most back gardens begins with a terrace or patio for sitting and outdoor dining. The outer edges of the terrace might flow from the corners of the house or from the center of windows or some other architectural feature. In one design for clients, I started paving a stone patio about eighteen inches away from the foundation, leaving space to plant a bed with fragrant perennials and annuals and even evergreen shrubs for year-round interest.

After you have established a broad design for the back patio, work out how the side paths will link up with it. One approach is to have the paths come around the corners of the house and lead you to the patio; another is to run them out to a distant arbor and link that to the patio with a third path. When you know where the paths will go, you can design a three- or four-foot-wide perennial and shrub border around the patio to create a feeling of enclosure.

Steps onto the patio are perfect places for container gardening. You can plant large terra-cotta or stone pots with fragrant annuals and perennials, or with patio tomatoes, herbs, and runner beans, which can climb bamboo poles set into the potted soil.

All of these new ways of thinking about planting near the house will make you feel much more involved with your gardens. Because you have new ways to use new plants in new places, you will become excited about your property and the many ways you can enhance it.

CHAPTER 7
ENHANCING A SMALL GARDEN

Paths can help you create all kinds of new looks in a small garden, but the central principle to keep in mind is coherence. Be sure the paths flow easily and logically from one to the next. Vary materials to increase the sense of size, but don't overdo it, or your garden will become a hodgepodge of opposing materials and styles. Use restraint, but don't be boring.

Varying the experience of your visitors is the key to making a small garden look and feel larger than it really is. Paths can lead you from sun to filtered shade to deep shade back into sun and on to shade; they can lead you up and down and around and under and through; they can introduce you to a shrub-and-perennial border and then to grass and then to a patch of wildflowers and then to a formal area. Vary the plantings and you vary the feeling. Add detail with garden ornament, sculpture, trompe l'oeil and forced-perspective trelliswork, gates, furniture, planted containers, and maybe even running water, all of which

The short distance between a sidewalk and a front door can provide the site for a wonderfully colorful garden built around a curving brick path. Small trees are appropriate in this kind of space.

can be incidents along a path or its destination. If you knit all these varied experiences together along a well-defined path of logically varied materials, your little garden will feel like a world apart.

The first step is to divide the space you now have into two or three smaller spaces. This might mean completely screening off one of the spaces with a fence or a tall hedge and partially screening off the others. Hedges made of boxwood, lavender, or daylilies, which you can see over, can be an excellent way to separate one garden space from the next without creating a feeling of claustrophobia. Paths that link these spaces together are centrally important to enhancing that sense of greater space.

STRAIGHT PATHS

Take advantage of the longest view you have with at least one long straight path that allows the eye to travel as far as possible. One small garden I saw in England was only eighteen feet wide — that is, as wide as the back of a row house — and fifty feet long. The designer ran a two-foot-wide path right down the center to create two eight-foot-wide beds on either side. A single step a third of the way and another two thirds of the way along the path gave people the feeling that they were entering new gardens, thereby creating the illusion of greater space. (If the designer had put little sections of fence with gates where the two steps were, that would have further increased the feeling of space.) At the far end of the path was a false door into the back fence, giving the impression that this garden was just the first of many.

Borrowing the view at the end of a long path is another way to increase the illusion of distance. On my property, we put in a long lawn path that ran between two perennial beds to a row of trees and brush, which hid a wonderful view of mountains in the distance, beyond a meadow. We uprooted all the brush at the end of the path and high-pruned the trees, so now we can see far into the distance from anywhere along the path, through a frame of tree trunks and a gazebo. You might have a view of a distant church, a city skyline, or a neighbor's pond from your garden. Take advantage of the longest view by making your paths follow the sight line to those distant objects, and your garden will feel bigger.

Varying materials and their width can create the illusion of greater space, and fences, hedges, and gates promise that there is more garden beyond. Tall evergreens and trees beyond the gate increase the sense of distance.

FENCING AND WALLS

Fences can help separate your property from that of your neighbors and in the process give your garden the illusion of greater space and definition. In a particularly fine example, a Massachusetts designer fenced off the sides and back of his client's property to create two eight-foot-wide side gardens and a fifteen-foot-wide back garden. (The neighbors' houses were only eight feet from the back of the fencing on all three sides.) To reduce the massiveness of the seven-foot-high fences along the side gardens, he put trellises against them and planted vines that would wind in and out, creating a wall of greenery.

Next he set in meandering stepping-stone paths. On one side of the house the path leads through richly underplanted birches and shadblows to a grape arbor at the back. The overhang of the arbor screens the view of the neighbors' houses and creates an intimate inner space. When you sit under the arbor, you face the length of the side garden you've just walked through, and because of the trees, the underplantings, and a gate in the fence at the far end, you feel as though you are in quite a large space, though in fact you are only eight feet away from a neighbor's house. The straight path and its view, in combination with the fence, arbor, and skillful planting, have created a view into a long, narrow little world.

This narrow space has been enlivened by the refined use of brick and gravel to create a beautiful path. The general tone is enhanced by window boxes, a fine gate, and the restrained green-and-white color scheme.

Even a very narrow passageway between the garage and the side of the house can be made into a wonderful garden. The long straight path leads the eye to the statue of Saint Fiacre, the patron saint of gardeners, and to the small arbor above it.

PAVING MATERIALS

The designer of this same garden also provided a good example of how to alter paving materials to increase the feeling of space. When you step out of the grape arbor and turn toward the back door of the house, you walk through a gap in a stone wall that separates the arbor from an outdoor dining area. You are still walking on stepping stones, but now they are surrounded by beach pebbles rather than the evergreen groundcovers used in the side garden. Between this stepping-stone path and the back fence is the dining area, which has a small table and four chairs placed on granite cobble. Overhead is another arbor, this one with flowering vines. By changing the paving surface from stepping stones to cobble, the designer divided the area up visually but not physically, thereby enlarging the feeling of space.

THE CONCEPT OF CENTERS

Another way to look at this example is to see how the designer has created three different centers, each with its own mood, within a very confined space. First is the birch-and-shadblow copse, which echoes the New England woods with its vertical lines and the interplay between the evergreen shrubs and groundcovers and the white bark of the birches. Next is the vine-covered arbor at the end of the copse, which is enclosed, completely shady and sheltering. Then comes the cobbled dining area, with furniture at its center. These three centers — three separate experiences — are all contained within a garden walk that takes no more than thirty paces to traverse.

Yet another way to look at this is to think about the prepositions that describe the walk through this garden. You walk *through* the gate and *under* its arch and *along* the fence and *between* the trees and *on* the stepping stones. You then go *into* the arbor to sit *on* a chair *under* the grapes. If you walk *through* the gap in the stone wall, you step *onto* the granite cobble to sit *on* another chair *under* another arbor for lunch, after which you might go *around* the corner of the house and *into* the other side garden. All these different prepositions point to the different experiences the garden provides.

This garden has an itinerary that offers a wide range of experiences and feelings in a very short period of time and in a very short distance. By articulating

Frame the longest view in a small garden with an arbor pathway down its length, and increase the feeling of size by varying the paving materials and plantings around it.

Here a wide gravel path narrows quickly to create the illusion of greater length. The designer has skillfully foreshortened space.

the direction you are meant to take as you explore its variety, the path gradually unfolds the meaning of the garden.

Curving Paths

A curving path planted densely to just above eye level on both sides can also increase the feeling of space in a small garden. By preventing you from seeing the end of the path, the curves obscure the edges of the garden and screen the final destination from view. You feel enclosed and held in just a bit of suspense.

This feeling of suspense is particularly useful at a garden entrance. For instance, the designer of a garden I saw in Georgia laid a stone carpet that was eight feet wide at the entrance but narrowed over a distance of no more than fifteen or twenty feet to a path of single stepping stones, which disappeared around a corner planted densely with shrubs. The result was a kind of optical illusion that foreshortened space. By combining the curve in the path with tall shrubs to hide the destination — the rest of the garden — the designer created the illusion that the garden was much larger than it really was.

To see how you might use this principle in your own small garden, walk around the edges of your property and think about how you can screen off and enclose your garden from your neighbors' view. Once you have created a feeling of enclosure, you can use a curving path to help increase the sense of space.

A meandering path is also useful for suggesting that a small woodland is much larger than it seems. For example, find a pair of large trees that can act as a portal, creating a feeling of entrance. Another pair might serve as an exit onto the lawn. Now go into the woods and use bright forester's tape to mark all the interesting elements you find: a mossy boulder, the decaying trunk of a grand old tree; a view into a neighbor's garden or field; a stand of ferns; a slope that goes down to a sunny area where you might sit. Then, using shears and a saw, cut a sinuous and meandering path through the woods. Vary the experience further by cutting branches very high in some places and low in others and by widening and narrowing the path as you go along. Take the path past your points of interest, and then set out an old chair or bench in the sunny spot. If the path meanders and there is a lot to see along the way, a half-acre of woods out back can become a richly varied part of your garden.

CHAPTER 8
SITING PERENNIAL BEDS

You may have planted perennials at any number of places on your property: along one or both sides of a stone wall or fence, along one side of a hedge, around a terrace or patio, or beside your house, the garage, or an outbuilding. But there are many not-so-obvious places where perennial gardens look wonderful, and paths, in combination with fences and walls, can offer help in finding them.

No matter where you put a perennial bed, of course, you need to keep in mind that many perennials and shrubs need at least six hours of direct sunlight a day. The bed must also be at least twenty feet away from the branch tips of any large trees if the plants are to flourish. Shade-tolerant perennials should be planted under fruit trees, which have less aggressive surface roots than many hardwoods, or under trees such as black cherries, oaks, and locusts, which have

---

Here a sloping lawn has been replaced by a pleasing garden built around a gravel path, which flows down from the back of the house through a series of simply constructed terraces.

The proportions of all the elements in this garden are determined by the gazebo at the far end: the straight central path is the same width as the structure, and the perennial beds are one and a half times as wide.

deeper taproots. Trees with matted surface roots, such as beech, maple, birch, ash, and even ornamentals like Japanese tree lilacs, will make shade gardening a very trying experience.

PERENNIALS AND THE FRONT PRIMARY PATH

As you have seen, a path from the sidewalk or the garage to the front door can make a good spine for a perennial garden. If the front walkway is in full sun, you might plant pairs of small trees such as *Stewartia pseudocamellia* every twenty-five feet or so along the path to add interest and structure to the beds.

You might also consider taking out a few, most, or even all of the shrubs in your foundation planting, adding compost and peat moss to the spent soil, and replacing the shrubs with large-scale and long-blooming perennials. If you lay twenty-four-inch-square pieces of bluestone along the outer edge of the bed, they will keep lawn grass from creeping in among the perennials and act as a path along the front of the house. Or you might take up your whole front lawn and put in a huge perennial and shrub garden like English cottage gardens, complete with a picket fence running along the sidewalk.

A designer outside Washington, D.C., created a wonderful perennial and shrub garden that greets guests and the owner daily with an exuberance of color, form, and texture. The modest suburban home had about fifty feet of lawn that sloped gently down to the sidewalk, with a concrete walkway running up the lawn and between foundation planting to the front door. The first thing the designer did was take out the walkway, which she eventually replaced with bluestone, a far more interesting material. Because a sloping lot is never wholly satisfactory for setting off a house, she put a two-foot-high stone retaining wall about twenty feet out from the house and backfilled the area up to the foundation with topsoil to make it flat. Along the front of the wall she created a ten-foot-wide sloping garden, which met the final twenty feet of lawn that ran out to the sidewalk.

The designer then laid a six-foot-wide bluestone path from the sidewalk to the front door, taking its width from the width of the portico over the door. Bluestone steps help people walk up the sloping section of garden and through the gap in the wall. Beside the steps she planted a pair of dogwoods (any small flowering trees would be appropriate), and under them and along the length of the sloping garden she set in evergreen shrubs, perennials, bulbs, and annuals.

In the top portion of the front garden, the designer replaced the foundation planting with a bed of mixed perennials, evergreens, and annuals that came about six feet out from the wall of the house. The area between this bed and the top of the stone wall was planted in lawn grass, and one section serves as a lawn path to invite visitors to wander into a shady perennial garden at the side of the house. There a stepping-stone path leads on to the back gardens.

This garden is a wonderful example of how varied and interesting an experience it can be to arrive at someone's front door. If you really pay attention to what is in bloom, whether in spring, summer, or fall, the walk up to this house can take twenty minutes.

Relating Shapes and Proportions

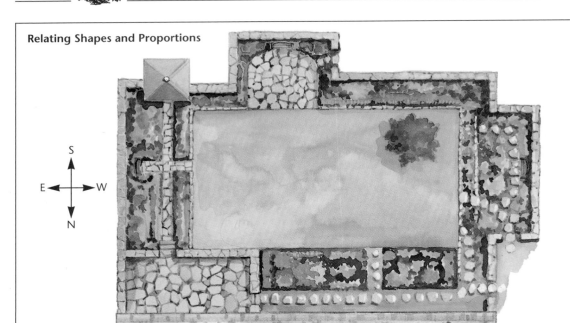

S

E ← → W

N

All the lines of the gardens, the walls, and the paths are parallel or perpendicular to the south side of this house. The paths within the walls, in combination with the walls themselves, give rise to any number of appropriate places for perennial borders.

PLANTING THE SIDE GARDENS

All of the information about side gardens given in earlier chapters is relevant to siting a perennial border, whether in sun or shade. Here, then, is a different idea, based on a large garden I visited in the Berkshire Hills of Massachusetts. The dimensions can be altered to fit your own space, of course.

The designer first set aside an area roughly forty feet long and sixty feet wide on the south side of the client's house, establishing the edges by constructing a stone wall that ran south from one corner of the house, turned west for about fifty feet, and then turned north to the other corner of the house. That is, the dimensions and the shape of the garden came directly from the dimensions and shape of the side of the house. Then he laid a two-foot-wide stone carpet parallel to but five feet inside the stone wall and planted a perennial and shrub border in the space between the two.

These curving perennial beds have been cut out of the lawn along the side of a house. Because the path between the beds is uniform in width, it looks like a path rather than a bit of lawn between two unrelated gardens. The beds were planted around existing small trees.

The next step was to do something few designers do — he added a three-foot-wide perennial bed on the *inside* of the stone carpet. This second bed makes all the difference, because it puts the garden visitor inside rather than at the edge of the garden. A square of lawn at the center was left intact, to provide a green foil for the perennials in the adjacent beds. The raised stone terrace that runs along the wall of the house provides a wonderful vantage point from which to look down onto this three-sided garden.

Naturally, your house might not be the same size as this one, but the idea is still a good one. If the side of your house is thirty feet wide, you can create a six-

Planting Within an Ell

An ell can be a fine place for a perennial garden. Use this model when thinking about how to take advantage of this private and sheltered spot to create a fragrance garden. The gaps between the stepping stones add to the informality of the space. Trees increase the feeling of enclosure, and planted pots add detail.

foot-wide bed with the stone carpet running through it, or you might choose gravel, brick, or stepping stones. You could replace the stone wall with a split-rail fence or a solid wooden fence, or plant a yew or lilac hedge as a backdrop. The point is to work with this model and any others you encounter. Alter them — change their dimensions and shapes and make the ideas work for your house and your style of gardening.

PLANTING AN ELL

Many houses include a door that leads into a sheltered ell of the house. This door can be seen as the beginning of a path through a new garden based on the dimensions of the architecture. For example, you might make a square or rectangular garden by taking up the sod in between the end of the house and the door, or between the side of the ell and a major window, a setback, or some other structural element.

Gardens within an ell offer all kinds of opportunities for perennials. You might pave a stone terrace in the middle of the space and plant shrubs and perennials around all four sides of it, leaving gaps where paving stones invite people into the space from the house and the adjacent lawn. Or you might run a gravel path from the door through a rose-covered trellis into an herb garden protected by the long side of the house. The garden can become a hub from which two or three other paths lead to other parts of your property.

PLANTING AROUND A SWIMMING POOL

If you have a swimming pool surrounded by lawn, you might be inspired to create a poolside garden by one of my own designs. The twenty-by-forty-foot pool

Planting Perennials Around a Pool

Planting a hedge around a swimming pool creates all kinds of possibilities for perennial gardens. Further additions add even more interest to the pool area. The line of the hedge can be broken up with a section of split-rail fence, and gates, benches, and smaller paths can introduce the unexpected to such a garden.

A richly planted perennial garden might work well if it is designed around a fieldstone and river-rock path leading from the ell of a house to existing trees.

near my client's house was surrounded by a six-foot-wide concrete coping and then lawn, with no visual interruptions other than an arbor near the north side of the pool. Taking the coping as an important measurement, I left six feet of lawn between the coping and the next element of my design, a three-foot-wide bed that I filled with perennials. Along the back of the bed I planted a four-foot-high yew hedge, to set the pool area off from the rest of the property. The hedge was designed with four breaks or gaps, one on each side, so that people coming from the nearby stone terrace or from the lawn could easily walk into the enclosed pool area.

The perennial bed not only provided a wonderful garden to look at while swimming or sunbathing, but it also added to the feeling of protection and privacy. To add even further to that feeling, I planted several crab-apple trees between the back of the hedge and the driveway. The lawn path between the pool and the flowers tended to expand the feeling of spaciousness, and it offered a cool green pathway as an alternative to the hotter and harder concrete coping. The whole experience of being in the pool and looking up and out at the perennials was a most satisfying result of this design.

PLANTING AROUND A PATIO

Suppose that your patio has an opening six feet wide at the center that leads into your backyard. One attractive way to add perennials would be to place two long beds on either side of a path that leads straight out across your lawn.

If you like this idea, attach a fifty- or sixty-foot-long piece of twine to each corner of the patio opening and then draw them out to their farthest extent, making sure they are six feet apart at both ends. Imagine that the six-foot-wide panel of lawn between those two strings is a lawn path and the strings represent the inner edges of the perennial beds.

How wide those beds will be is up to you, but look carefully at your lawn for clues as to what width would be appropriate. Perhaps the beds should be nine feet wide and backed with a hedge, or maybe they should be the same as the path, six feet wide, with shrubs interplanted. You might want to curve the edges at the far side from the path, and those curves might suggest the shapes of other beds across other lawn paths.

Once you've decided to run that wide lawn path between beds, you might want to experiment with ways to plant around it. You could consider making a series of two or three beds on either side that are parallel with, rather than perpendicular to, the back of the house. This would enable you to run secondary lawn paths between the beds toward side gardens and paths.

And what might go at the far end of the path off the patio? A gazebo? A single wonderful tree? A great big planted pot on a large flat stone set into the lawn? Any number of solutions suggest themselves.

Free-form beds set into brick paving offer a wide variety of places for perennials, shrubs, small trees, and planted pots.

Designing a Perennial Garden for Shade

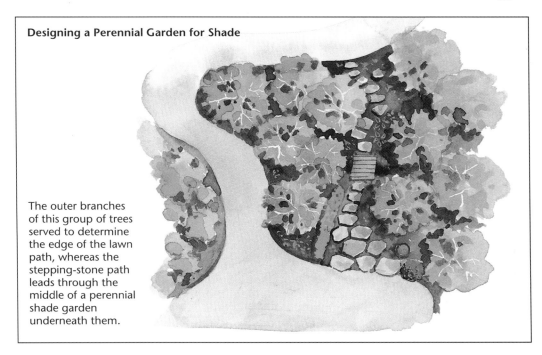

The outer branches of this group of trees served to determine the edge of the lawn path, whereas the stepping-stone path leads through the middle of a perennial shade garden underneath them.

PLANTING A SHADE GARDEN

When I created a shady spring garden under a group of wild plum trees that were growing on our property, I established the outer edge of the bed simply by following the dripline of the trees. The stone wall behind the trees, which marks our property line, became the back edge of the bed.

Once I had established the shape of the bed, I set a stepping-stone path through the copse so that we could walk among the trees and the shrubs and perennials we had planted under them. That path through the middle helped not only with the maintenance but with the planting scheme, encouraging us to plant low groundcovers near the path and taller and taller perennials as we worked toward the back. In the part of the bed between the stepping stones and the lawn, we built up to the middle area and then planted lower and lower plants as we got toward the lawn. By paying attention to the dripline and the path, we were able to create a shade-loving perennial and shrub garden that settled right into the landscape and related to the shapes and proportions of nearby gardens.

CHAPTER 9
PUTTING IT
ALL TOGETHER

If you have a garage, a small garden shed, or an outbuilding on your property, that structure might just be the place to start your garden design. It certainly was for my wife and me.

Our garden shed sits across the driveway from our two-hundred-year-old farmhouse in Vermont. A hundred years ago, the owners moved the shed, a twelve-by-eighteen-foot building made of barnboard, to its current position so they could use it as an outbuilding for the farm. In a sense, the shape and materials of the shed helped us decide where to put our herb garden, two hedges, a peony garden, pots, and any number of garden ornaments. In a larger sense, the design for the gardens around this small building had a ripple effect, influencing the design of all the gardens on our property. You could say that we started with an easy part of the design and built toward the more complex. There was never a master plan for the whole; instead, one thing led to another.

The proportions and position of this hundred-year-old garden shed helped us create a coherent herb garden with a grape arbor and sitting area. Small outbuildings and even a garage can be a starting point for good ideas for new gardens.

Designing a Garden Near a Shed

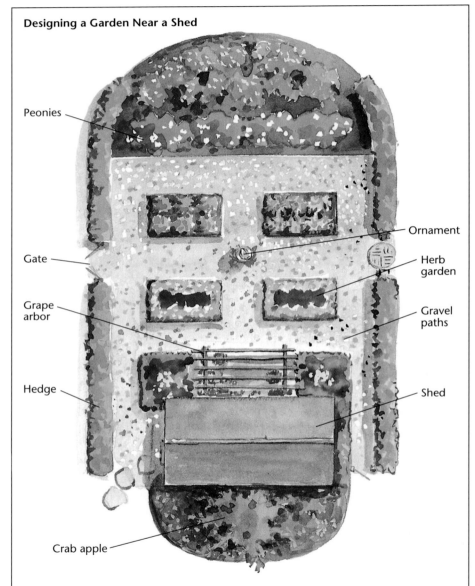

Peonies

Gate

Grape arbor

Hedge

Crab apple

Ornament

Herb garden

Gravel paths

Shed

The tool shed in our garden gave rise to a simple plan for a hedged herb garden. By paying attention to the proportions and shapes of small outbuildings on your property, you can create private and satisfying gardens that have their own distinctive character.

PLACING THE MAJOR ELEMENTS FIRST

When we began, we knew that we wanted a grape arbor somewhere in the garden, and the back side of the shed seemed a perfect place for it. The shed would shelter it from the predominant west wind, and the arbor would provide shade in July and August and give us a place to plant *Clematis paniculata,* the fall-blooming clematis, as well as grapevines.

So without worrying about what the next step would be, we had our friend build an arbor for us, based on the shed's materials and proportions. The long side of the arbor parallels the shed's long wall and is centered on it, and our friend placed the inside of the top deck, on which the vines rest, only one foot away from the shed, so the two structures are closely related. Because the shed is made of weathered barnboard, we decided that the uprights that would hold the deck should be rustic posts cut from black locust trees across the road. In the ground, the uprights will last for decades. Once the arbor was built, we paved the surface underneath with fieldstones laid tightly together to form a surface for a bench and a few chairs.

USING PATHS TO MAKE DESIGN DECISIONS

This is when paths began to play their role. When we sat under the arbor, we wanted to look out onto a garden. We decided on a four-quadrant herb garden, and we used the shed to help us determine proportions, so it wouldn't overwhelm the garden. The outer edges of the beds would be parallel with the ends of the shed; the main path would be half the shed's width; the subordinate paths would be one third the shed's width. These decisions did not follow hard-and-fast rules but came from paying attention to the look of the garden in relation to the shed. We wanted the two to look good together.

Once we had laid out strings to determine where the beds and paths would go, we sat down under the arbor and looked around, only to see our car in the driveway. We thought how nice it would be to be able to sit in a little enclosed garden without seeing the house or the car, and that's when we decided to plant hedges. I had just read an article on *Viburnum prunifolium* as a fine hedging plant; it has shiny, leathery leaves, white flowers in May, black berries for the birds in late summer, brilliant red leaves in October, and a willingness to take

The paths into the herb garden are related to other paths in the area and link the garden around the shed to other garden spaces, making a coherent whole.

shearing. Using string, we laid out the lines of two hedges along the outer edges of the two side paths in such a way that they formed entrances to the herb garden at either end of the shed. We also left a break in each hedge where the cross-path leads through the center of the garden.

When we laid out the central path in the herb garden and stood at the north end looking south, we realized that we had just determined the location of the entrance steps into another garden area we had planned, a shady rock garden. When we built those steps many weeks later, they showed us where the path for the long perennial borders would go, and that showed us where to put the entrance to the woodland garden, and that showed us... In a literal way, all the paths, and thereby the designs for all the gardens, emanated from our first design decision. Paths help a lot.

LETTING PATHS DETERMINE MATERIALS

After we laid out the four quadrants of the herb garden with string, we cut the edges of the existing sod with a straight-nosed spade and then lifted the sod to create the four beds. We added a great deal of sand and compost to the soil and stepped back to look at our handiwork. Right away we realized that leaving so much lawn within such a small garden and between the hedges would call for a lot of tedious mowing and edging. As sumptuous as the grass looked between the quadrants, we didn't have time to keep it looking right in such a small space. So we took up all the sod and a further two inches of topsoil between and around the four beds, laid down woven black plastic groundcloth, and covered it with two inches of $\frac{3}{8}$-inch peastone. Now the paths needed no edging, no mowing, and, as it turned out over the years, very little maintenance. Furthermore, because all the paths outside the herb garden were made of lawn, when we stepped onto the peastone we heard the crunch and saw a different-colored surface underfoot. Both helped announce that we had entered a new garden area.

USING PATHS TO PLACE PLANTS

Once the four beds were ready for planting, we decided we wanted to mark the center of each one with a strong, large-scale plant that would be there year-round. We decided on *Inula magnifica,* so we ordered four of them. With these in mind, we decided to plant a relatively low collection of herbs around them. Because the shed is so rustic, we didn't feel we needed to plant symmetrically, especially since we had linked the beds with the *Inula,* so we designed each bed independently, repeating some plants here and there just to keep some semblance of order. Each quadrant contained traditional herbs — sage, parsley, thyme, oregano, summer savory, lavender, and the like — and in early June we set out annual herbs such as lemon verbena and rosemary. To enhance the feeling of enclosure, we planted a low hedge of hybrid peonies at the end of the herb garden, parallel to and along the edge of the lower path.

The shed and the arbor also gave us places for perennials and vines. Near the northern entrance to the herb garden we planted a climbing hydrangea, which looks good all year long against the wall of the shed. The path forces visitors to go up close to it to see the flowerheads and the leaves. On the other end

The hedge and the end of the garden shed make a logical entrance for the path into the herb garden, and the path itself suggested the gate, the planted pots, and the edges of the herb beds. The end of a path is always a good place to put a birdbath or another large garden ornament.

of the shed we planted male and female bittersweet vines. On the opposite side of the shed from the arbor, we planted a red-leaved 'Royalty' crab apple, underplanting it with *Geranium macrorrhizum* 'Spessart'.

In the south corner created by the arbor and the shed we planted a mass of *Macleaya cordata* that grows seven or eight feet high, interplanted with four- to five-foot pink Asiatic lilies. On the north corner we planted bee balm to attract hummingbirds to our sitting area. By placing these two invasive plants within the confines of the paved paths, the shed, and the paving under the arbor, we were able to contain them without a lot of effort.

The central path through the garden provides a good place for a sundial, whereas the side entrance calls for ornamental gates. This path, made of gravel which crunches underfoot, leads to stone steps into a shady rock garden.

USING PATHS TO PLACE ORNAMENTS

Once the gardens and hedges were planted, we were free to add details, an element that is especially important in a small garden, where visual variety contributes to the illusion of spaciousness. We looked to the paths for clues as to their placement. First we purchased a sundial and a pedestal, placed it in the center of the herb garden, and planted around the base with *Teucrium*. We placed my grandmother's birdbath at the end of one of the paths and a large potted *Brugmansia* 'Ecuador Pink' at the end of another path. We bought gates for three of the four entrances and suspended them from black locust posts like the ones

The rustic grape arbor, as wide as the garden shed, provides a place to sit in the herb garden. The posts, cut from dead black locusts on the property, support both the arbor and the gates.

we used for the arbor uprights. A friend gave us a matched pair of granite fenceposts, and we used them for the fourth entrance.

The base of the gateposts became a logical place for terra-cotta containers filled with wonderful plant combinations. At either end of the viburnum hedges, we planted large pots with blue lacecap hydrangeas and *Artemisia* 'Silver Brocade'. Next to the gates we planted pots of various sizes with *Fuchsia* 'Gartenmeister' and *Helichrysum petiolare* 'Limelight'. At the base of the arbor uprights we set out large pots of Asiatic lilies or of annual diascias. For the past few years we have placed a seven-foot potted *Brugmansia* tree in the herb garden; the fragrance from its nine-inch-long yellow trumpets — sometimes there are as many as seventy on the tree at once — fills the air for weeks.

TYING IT ALL TOGETHER

Once we had created the paths through the herb garden, we immediately saw how the cross-path would help us locate steps up into a shady rock garden. That path in turn pointed the way to the long path between two perennial gardens to a gazebo. The gazebo gave us the idea for a rebar tunnel from the woodland garden, and so on and on.

In sum, we started with the easiest problem. Success with solving that gave us the clues we needed to send our garden design, with its related paths, out into a full acre and a half.

PHOTO CREDITS

Karen Bussolini: vi–1, 2, 93

Marge Garfield: 12, 56, 110, 120

Gordon Hayward: 14, 21, 48, 100, 114, 116, 118

Margaret Hensel/Positive Images: 61, 71

Saxon Holt: 22, 24, 76, 85

Jerry Howard/Positive Images: 7, 62, 66, 78, 83

Ivan Massar/Positive Images: 17, 95

Rick Mastelli: iii, 9, 30, 38, 43, 50, 54–55, 86, 96, 108

Jerry Pavia: 5, 8, 19, 26, 60, 70, 81, 88, 91, 92, 98, 103

Michael L. Selig: 59, 64, 74, 80, 106

Stephen R. Swinburne: 117

Titles available in the Taylor's Weekend Gardening Guides series:

Organic Pest and Disease Control	$12.95
Safe and Easy Lawn Care	12.95
Window Boxes	12.95
Attracting Birds and Butterflies	12.95
Water Gardens	12.95
Easy, Practical Pruning	12.95
The Winter Garden	12.95
Backyard Building Projects	12.95
Indoor Gardens	12.95
Plants for Problem Places	12.95
Soil and Composting	12.95
Kitchen Gardens	12.95
Garden Paths	12.95
Easy Plant Propagation	12.95

At your bookstore or by calling 1-800-225-3362

Prices subject to change without notice